The Complete Guide To
BUYING A PROPERTY IN SPAIN

Anthony I Foster

CREATIVE MEDIA ASSOCIATES SPAIN Málaga

2012

The Complete Guide to Buying a Property in Spain
by Anthony I Foster

First published September 1994
Tenth edition published July 2012 by
Creative Media Associates Spain
Calle Puerta del Mar 9
29780 Nerja
Málaga
Spain

A **www.creativespain.com** production
for
www.propertysearchspain.co.uk

ISBN: 978-84-940270-1-7

Typeset in Adobe Garamond Pro
by Creative Media Associates Spain

Printed in the UK by Lightning Source UK Ltd
Milton Keynes, MK11 3LW

Acknowledgements

IN researching and writing this book, I have been advised and helped by a good many people, many of whom prefer to remain in the background. You know who you are and I thank you for your patience and professional insights.

I would be remiss, however, not to acknowledge the advice and input of Maria Jose Cobos Mayorga - an accountant and *Gestor* in Nerja – the *Notario*, notary, in Nerja, Banco Sabadell bank, insurers MAPFRE, property sales and rental specialists Teamstar Holiday Rentals, part of Team Group the *Ayuntamiento de Nerja,* which is my local Town Hall, the local property rates office *Recaudacion Provincial de Málaga,* the local water board, the electricity supplier Endesa, and telephone company Movistar, which is a brand of Telefónica.

All provided information in the knowledge that while this book might cite examples from their own experience, products and services it makes no endorsement of anyone or any company in particular.

Great care and attention has been take in updating this book, but any errors will be entirely of my own making and should not reflect on anyone who provided information.

Most of all, I would like to thank my wife who has had to put up with me *dando la luz* to a long overdue tenth edition of this guide over a period when a flurry of market and legislative changes, not least a change of government, kept shifting the target.

BUYING IN SPAIN? READ THIS FIRST!

THIS GUIDE helps to avoid problems when buying property in Spain. I also offer an After-Sales Service. During 30 years of living and working in Spain, I have built a network of tried and trusted estate agents and other professionals in most coastal areas of the mainland and the islands. These include: Costa del Sol, Costa Blanca, Costa de la Luz, Mallorca, Menorca and the Canary Islands. I place this at your disposal. If you intend to buy, I can contact an agent in your area of choice and ask them to send you information. When you wish to visit, I will ask them to meet you at the airport or wherever. If you wish, they will arrange accommodation.

You may contact me in Nerja, Málaga province, Spain, at either of these numbers: **Telephone:** +34 95 252 3695   **Mobile:** +34 629 577445
If you wish to speak to me personally, call between 17.00 and 19.30 hours United Kingdom time, Monday to Friday. Or you may fax or email: **fax:** +34 95 252 3695 **email:** info@propertysearchspain.co.uk

Mail should go to my UK office:
Property Search Spain
Sheraton House
Castle Park
Cambridge
CB3 0AX
UNITED KINGDOM

The UK office can also take calls and faxes in my absence.
tel: +44 (0)1223 380145   **Fax:** +44 (0)1223 370040

Ordering additional copies of this book

Through local bookshops, online retailers, and direct from either
www.propertysearchspain.co.uk or **www.spainpropertyinvestor.com**

CONTENTS

NOTES

FIGURES

In Spain, one hundred thousand Euros and fifty Euro cents would be written as: **100.000,50 Euros**

But in this book, we use the United Kingdom and US convention, so the same figure would be written as: **100,000.50 Euros**

Introduction

SO YOU have arrived in Spain looking forward to the sunshine and it is 'All Systems Go' in the search for your dream home. But as you sip your first chilled drink, heed a few words of well meant advice from an old pro, so to speak. **Do not leave your brains in the left-luggage locker at the airport!** Many have done just that and lived to regret it. Many more have heeded the warning and avoided numerous pitfalls to settle into new homes and fulfilling, sun-drenched lives with the minimum of fuss.

The media thrive on tragic stories about people who went in search of a Spanish Shangri-La only to lose life savings through the wiles of unscrupulous developers or estate agents. Maybe they met someone in a bar who had property for sale, only to discover too late that the friendly local did not own it, or there were enormous debts on the property.

More recently, you may have seen heart rending pictures of retired couples in tears as the bulldozers moved in to demolish homes built on land they were assured was zoned for residential building but proved not to be. The entire Costa del Sol town of Marbella was brought to the brink of ruin and thousands of homes there were declared illegal after decades of unlawful construction sanctioned by local politicians and bureaucrats in cahoots with developers. Even the Hollywood star Antonio Banderas, a son of Málaga province, ran into planning difficulties with his beachfront home in Marbella. So what price an easy ride for foreigners, you may ask.

With more than 30 years' experience behind me, I am acutely aware of what can happen, which is why I first wrote this guide in 1994 and update it regularly to keep up with changing laws, practices, trends and events.

With the Spanish housing market now on its knees and with more than a million — some say two million - unsold new properties hanging over everything, there has never been a better time to find bargains. Plenty of savvy investors and nesters are doing just that, but need to be doubly smart when so many sellers – and that includes the Spanish banks - are desperate to get properties off their hands.

What I can say though, is that for every harrowing tale of fortunes lost and homes confiscated, there are hundreds of thousands of satisfied expatriate house owners who bought trouble-free and are enjoying their lives or regular holidays in Spain. This book will help you to join their satisfied ranks and spare you from making expensive blunders.

Before going into the fine detail, here are a few key tips to fix firmly in mind from the outset.

Everyone is selling or knows someone who is: Just about everyone you meet professes to be an expert and apparently does a bit of property selling. Mention that you are in Spain to buy property and the waiter will tell you of a friend with something at a very good price, or knows someone who will help. Maybe you get into conversation with a local who will inevitably know someone looking to sell or may try to sell you their own property. Do not get involved. If anything goes wrong, and it probably will, you will have no comeback whatsoever.

Everyone is an expert: Spain is full of bar-room lawyers who profess to know it all about property, tax, and so on. Ignore them. At best, you get only half-truths and a lot of incorrect information.

Scout around: Unless you are on an inspection flight with a reputable agency and being met by their agents, spend time looking round the area. Find areas you like, note 'For Sale' signs, and contact the agency handling the sale. Ring the number on the sign: they will almost certainly speak English.

Check the estate agent: You will soon get a feel about an estate agent's trustworthiness, but it remains a good idea to ask if they are 'API registered' *(Agente de la Propiedad Inmobiliaria)*. These are registered with the province's professional College and should have placed a financial bond with them, giving you some protection if things go wrong. Or they may be GIPE registered (*Gestor Intermediario de Promociones y Edificaciones*), in which case they should be able to show you a certificate of their registration.

Remember, though, that there is no law regulating estate agents in Spain. Anyone can be an intermediary for selling property, so it would be difficult to hold an agent responsible if things go wrong.

If you **deal with an API or GIPE agent**, you are at least using someone who passed exams set by a professional body. However, this does not mean that you should not appoint a recommended lawyer when you find the property you wish to buy.

The absence of a 'For Sale' sign does not mean it is not for sale: the owners may not want a board. Ask estate agents if they have anything in your preferred area. Once again - and I cannot repeat this often enough – check they are **a registered API or GIPE agent.**

Details of their registration and relevant number should be on a sign outside the office, on the exterior, or in the window display. Look for a three or four figure number and ask for proof. If they cannot show it, walk away.

Hire a lawyer and pick the right one: Even dealing with a registered estate agent does not mean you are 100% safe. You simply must employ a lawyer.

There are lawyers and lawyers, so make sure you use one **recommended** by someone who previously used them to buy property successfully. Even then, it is a good idea to refer back to this book to see that your lawyer is doing the job properly and checking all the documentation that you will be reading about here.

Check in advance **what fees the lawyer will charge** for dealing with the legalities of the purchase. As a rule of thumb, lawyers in Spain charge between 1% - 1.5% of the purchase price.

Bear in mind that you will also have to pay transfer taxes, IVA value added tax, and Notary and Land Registry fees. This is described in Chapter 4.

So now you have found what you want to buy. What next? Before continuing, let me explain that the Spanish system is different from the English & Welsh, Scottish, and Irish ones.

In Spain, you are not dealing with solicitors who draw up and exchange contracts on completion. In Spain, all deeds for properties are drawn up by government appointed Public Notaries, *notarios*, highly experienced specialist lawyers. They are responsible for legalising many documents including title deeds known as *Escritura*s, Powers of Attorney, and so on.

On finding the property you wish to buy, a *Contrato de CompraVenta*, a contract of purchase and sale, is drawn up and a deposit is paid. This fixes the price, so **you cannot be trumped at the last minute by a higher bidder appearing from nowhere**.

This contract is completely binding on both parties. It includes the date of the final payment and the signing of the public *Escritura,* which is signed in the Notary's Office, witnessed by the *notario*, and legalised with his or her signature.

All parties involved must be present to sign the *Escritura* or must have appointed people with Power of Attorney to act on their behalf.

For example, if the property being purchased is in the names of a husband and wife as vendors and you and your wife are joint purchasers, then all four must be present or be represented by someone with a Power of Attorney drawn up in Spanish and notarised so that, say, a husband can sign for an absent wife or vice versa.

You have probably spent half a lifetime reaching this monumental decision. You are very excited at the prospect of owning your very own place in the sun. So please do not spoil it for yourself.

Give it plenty of thought before you proceed, and tread carefully. If you follow the guidelines laid down in this book, you that you should not go wrong.

Happy Home Hunting!

First Steps: Four Keys

SPAIN did not invent bureaucracy but has honed it to a frustrating art. If you are buying property and/or intending to live or work in Spain, then take these steps as soon as you arrive to save grief later. They are foundations to build a new life with less hassle than you might otherwise encounter. The four keys are: *Cuenta Bancaria* (Bank Account), NIE, *Residencia*, and *Empadronamiento*.

Key Step 1: Bank Account

You need a bank account in Spain to pay for property being sold in Euros and to pay standing orders for electricity, community fees, water, and property rates (IBI). Shop around as most banks charge a **fee on money transfers** to the account. This is typically 0.3%, which can be a lot for large transfers. I have usually managed to have this reduced to 0.2% and, in some cases, 0.1 %.

It is easy to open an account, particularly in coastal areas and islands, as most have multilingual staff. Present your passport, provide your address, sign contracts, and deposit a small sum.

Order a cheque book at the same time, as these come from head office and normally take up to four days. Request a 'hole in the wall' card too, as banks in Spain are normally closed after 14.00 hrs, and on Saturdays in summer months. **To speed money transfers**, ask for the full title of the Spanish bank, its postal address, IBAN number (this normally has the letters ES and two numbers), the ten digits of the sort code, the ten digits of the account number, and the Swift Telex Code for the bank. Request these when opening your account.

Most Spanish banks offer **internet banking**, clearly a boon to account holders based elsewhere and when frustratingly long queues can form in some Spanish bank branches. To speed matters, you can open an account as a non-resident then convert to a resident's account if you move to Spain.

Key Step 2: NIE

The *Numero de Identificacion Extranjero* (NIE), Foreigner Identification Number, is your ID number, and also your tax number if you will be tax resident. **You really must apply for your NIE certificate as soon as possible:** it takes up to a month to process.

Go personally to the nearest National Police Station with a *Departamento de Extranjeros*, Foreigners' Department, or give Power of Attorney to your lawyer or estate agent to do so on your behalf (but see '**Note well**' below). It is highly unlikely that a *Departmento de Extranjeros* will deal with you in any other language than Spanish: you are warned!

There, you present a completed application, a photocopy of it, and a form known as a Modelo 790. To pay for the NIE certificate, you or your lawyer should previously have taken the Modelo 790 to the bank to pay in 16 Euros for each application. This fee may change or could vary throughout Spain, so please use it only as a guide.

You will also need your passport and a photocopy of the passport page that bears your photograph. Your lawyer or estate agent should be able to supply all these forms.

If giving a lawyer or estate agent Power of Attorney to obtain your NIE number/s, you need your passports photocopied on official Notary's paper. This can be done at the Notary when you sign the Power of Attorney. The Notary sign theses and stamps them as authorised copies for about 4 Euros per passport.

Note well: If arranging an NIE from another country, check with your lawyer in Spain to see if he really can do this with a Power of Attorney, as rules change and can vary locally. At the time of writing the Spanish government is mulling over this issue and the future position is unclear,

In Nerja, where I live, a lawyer can apply for your NIE certificate only if you have had photocopies of the covers and every single page in your passport signed by a Public Notary in your country of residence and then sent, in the case of the United Kingdom, to the

UK Foreign Office to have an *Apostille,* a legal validation, attached to legalise these copies in Spain. You send these copies to your lawyer in Spain to apply for the NIE.

In other parts of Spain, they may accept a notarised photocopy of the passport page with your photograph on it.

Or you may **apply for an NIE at a Spanish Embassy or Consulate in your country of residence.** This takes longer than applying in Spain as they send application forms to Madrid who later post the NIE certificates to your home address. When applying for an NIE via a Spanish Consulate, allow **at least two months for delivery.**

Key Steps 3 & 4: Residencia & Empadronamiento

An EU directive which came into force in April 2006 states that a *Residencia* (proof of residency) is **not legally necessary for a citizen of an EU member country who has taken up permanent residence in Spain.** So you would only have to register on the electoral register in the town or village where you live and obtain a local *Certificado de Empadronamiento.*

Strictly speaking, it is unnecessary to have a *Residencia* if employed or self-employed and making your Social Security payments in Spain. But my advice is to obtain *Residencia,* as the Spanish authorities are constantly moving the goal posts.

The overworked Foreigners' Department will probably tell you that you do not need to have residency in Spain if you are working, but stand your ground and insist that you want to register as a resident.

However, as it is now so simple for EU citizens to obtain *Residencia,* my advice would be to go ahead and do it if you are planning to live in Spain for more than 183 days a year.

It just makes life simpler, does not affect your nationality, and you keep your passport. Advantages far outweigh any disadvantages and, despite the EU directive, it is still viewed as a legal requirement by some Spanish authorities. Try arguing with a Spanish policeman!

If you are of retirement age see Chapter 8

What you need: Obtaining a *Residencia* is comparatively simple for **citizens of member countries of the European Union (EU).** On arrival in Spain, you need the following documents and forms, some of which may be supplied by your lawyer or estate agent, who may also help to fill them in:

- An application form for each person and a photocopy of each application form.
- A Tax Form (Modelo 790). When it is filled in you must pay 10.20 Euros for each person applying. This is in Málaga province. The figure may vary elsewhere, so check with your lawyer.
- One passport sized photograph for each person applying (the photographs must be on a white background).
- The passports of each person applying, and a photocopy of each.
- A *Certificado de Empadronamiento* showing that you are registered on the electoral register in the town or village where you live.

The Spanish authorities no longer issue an ID card as a matter of course. They provide an A4 sheet of paper showing your details and NIE. **Keep this safe!** If this is all you have to prove your identity, you should still have your passport with you at all times to prove your identity to the Police/Guardia Civil. This might be necessary, say, if you were stopped by traffic control when driving, or if you had to prove identity when paying with a credit card or checking in at a hotel.

But to save you having to carry your passport, I advise going to the nearest Notary's office to ask them to **get the Notary to photocopy it onto official notarial paper.** They will then sign it to say that this is a copy of the original. The cost recently was approximately four Euros per passport. This copy should be accepted by the National Police, Municipal Police, and the Guardia Civil. It should also be accepted when paying with a credit card.

Where to apply: If you are an **EU national and are coming to work or to live in Spain for more than 183 days a year,** then you apply for the *Residencia* at the *Departmento de Extranjeros*, Foreigners' Department, at the same National Police offices in same way as for an *NIE*, and can do so at the same time if you wish. Your lawyer or the estate agent will be able to advise you where this is.

If you feel that going on your own will be too difficult, maybe because you do not speak Spanish very well, you should contact a *Gestoria Administrativa* who will send someone along with you to apply for the *Residencia*. Your lawyer or estate agent can put you in touch with a *Gestoria Administrativa* or may themselves be prepared to take you to obtain your *Residencia*.

When you go to the Foreigners' Department, you present all the documents plus one photograph for each person applying. They will stamp the application forms and attach photographs to their own copies before returning copies to you.

They may prepare your *Residencia* while you wait, which is certainly the case where I live, but in other locations you may well have to return at a later date to collect the *Residencia*. When you collect it you must present the document showing that you have paid for it, along with the application form.

A *Certificado de Empadronamiento* shows that you are registered on the *padrón*, **the electoral register** where you live. To obtain one from the local *Ayuntamiento*, Town Hall, present a copy of the *Escritura* title deeds for the home you have purchased, or for a property rental contract, along with your passport.

They may tell you that the Local Police will call at your property to ensure that you are living at this address. Once this has been done, they will register you on the *padrón* for local elections and you may then apply for the certificate that you will need in a number of situations.

Registering adds to the town's head count, so more public money comes its way. So registration is considered a civic duty. There is much resentment towards foreigners who settle in an area and use it services without registering. Be a good citizen!

Chapter 1: Buying a Resale Property

RESALE properties, i.e. second-hand, are the commonest purchase. Typically, a *Contrato de CompraVenta* **contract of purchase and sale** is drawn up, a deposit paid - normally 10% of agreed sale price - and the contract signed by vendor and purchaser.

Customs vary. I live in Nerja, Málaga province, where estate agents normally request a 'reservation payment' of 3,000 Euros towards that 10% deposit. A **'reservation contract'** is signed by both parties when the 3,000 Euros is paid. The property is thus reserved exclusively at the agreed price while your lawyer conducts searches, or to give sufficient time to arrange a mortgage.

If all goes to plan, the full *Contrato de CompraVenta* is drawn up and the balance of the 10% deposit becomes due in 15 to 21 days. If you do not pay the balance by the deadline, you forfeit the 3.000 Euros unless there was a legal obstacle to completion or if no mortgage was available. Any **deposit should be held by your lawyer** until he is sure everything is in order with the property before releasing funds to the vendor.

Both the Reservation Contract and the *Contrato de CompraVenta* should be drawn up by the estate agent or your lawyer. If by the agent, it is vital that your lawyer vets the contract before you sign and part with deposit money.

It is better to know about all **immediate and future expenses** before you buy. So before signing a *Contrato de CompraVenta*, find out:

- **Annual community fees**, *Gastos de la Comunidad*. On some *urbanizaciones* (complexes, housing estates) or *edificios* (apartment blocks), these can be up to 2,000 Euros per annum.
- Annual **Town Hall rates**, *Inmuebles y Bienes Inmobiliarias* (IBI).
- Approximate **costs of the *Escritura* deeds** and any other incidental charges.

Before signing contracts and paying a deposit, your lawyer must see the following:

• The *Escritura* **title deed**s to see that people claiming to be the owners really are.

• A *Nota Simple* **Land Registry document** showing legal owners and mortgages or other encumbrances on a property. This has a full description – bedrooms, bathrooms etc - and the surface area. These should match those on the *Escritura*. Otherwise it may mean any, some, or all of the following: sellers are not the owners; they have extended or altered property without permission; they failed to register a change, albeit approved; or the *Escritura* could not be registered.

Once your lawyer is satisfied, you move on to the *Contrato de CompraVenta* contract of purchase and sale. Before signing and paying a deposit you must ensure all the following issues are covered:

• **Price and payment terms** to be clearly written in the contract.

• **Purchasers are responsible for debts on the property** only from the day of the signing of the *Escritura* and the handing over of the keys. BUT your lawyer must see proof that any outstanding debts associated with a property have been paid up-to-date before signing the *Escritura* and making final payment. All debts in Spain are on the property, not the person. Charges to look out for include community fees, electricity, telephone, water - though this may be included in community fees - and *IBI* property rates.

• The **description of the property** in the *Contrato de CompraVenta* contract of purchase and sale must match that in both the *Escritura* and the *Nota Simple*. If not, the owners must show your lawyer a valid building licence for any extensions or alterations. They must accept, in writing in the contract, responsibility for the costs of declaring changes at the Notary's Office, including Land Registry fees. If there is no planning permission, your lawyer must ask the Town Hall to ascertain if the work can be legalised. If it can, the current owners will be responsible for all costs.

• The *Contrato de CompraVenta* contract of purchase and sale should show **full registration details from the Land Registry**: the *Finca* Number (The Land Registration No.); the book Number; and all other details. This information can be had from either the *Escritura* or the *Nota Simple*

• A section in the *Contrato de CompraVenta* contract of purchase and sale should be headed *Cargas,* charges, and should declare the property to be **'Free of Charges and Encumbrances'**. Any outstanding mortgage should show here. If you do not wish to take over the mortgage but would like it paid off, this should be taken up in the Conditions of Payment section of the contract as follows…

• The amount owed on the **existing mortgage**, including all cancellation costs, will be deducted from final payment. On the date of completion of the sale, your lawyer or estate agent will obtain the amount owed to the bank, and the cancellation costs for the Notary and Land Registry fees. The lawyer or agent will also arrange for a bank representative to attend the Notary's to sign a deed cancelling the mortgage. This normally happens on the same day and just prior to you signing the *Escritura* title deeds. The mortgage cancellation must be signed by the Notary prior to you signing your *Escritura*.

• There should be a clause headed *Arrendamiento,* covering any **tenants**, in the *Contrato de CompraVenta* contract of purchase and sale. This should declare the property free of sitting tenants.

• If property is **sold furnished**, normally the case for resale, a complete inventory should be drawn up and signed by both parties and annexed to the *CompraVenta*. This avoids nasty surprises when you return to sign the *Escritura* and, on checking the property, find no furniture. If the vendors are Spanish, the property may well be sold unfurnished. If so, ask for a list of what is being taken. I have had cases where property was sold unfurnished and vendors took not only furniture, curtains and light fittings, but also kitchen units, cooker, hob, refrigerator and washing machine. It is a good idea to visit the property just prior to completion to ensure that what has been agreed has been left.

• In general, Spanish tax laws oblige purchasers to **retain 3% of the sale value** declared on the *Escritura* for passing to the taxman. But if sellers are Spanish nationals, or are foreigners with *Residencia* (Resident) status in Spain, the retention does not apply. There are local variations. In some areas, there is no retention if vendors present just a current *Residencia* card. In others, a Notary will insist that vendors also present a certificate from the local tax office showing them to be tax resident in Spain, i.e. declaring all their taxes in Spain and not just filing tax returns of property taxes as a non-resident would Your lawyer will advise if you must retain the 3% or not. This is fully discussed in Chapter 12.

• The *Contrato de CompraVenta* contract of purchase and sale normally has a **double penalty clause** stating that if buyers do not complete the purchase on the date stated they will lose the deposit paid while vendors may put the property back on sale. If vendors do not complete on the date stated they must pay purchasers double the deposit paid. This ensures both parties are locked in and have considered all implications.

• One party may be taken **seriously ill just prior to completion**, and in my opinion it would be very harsh to impose penalties in such a case. So I would suggest that a further clause is inserted stating that, under Civil Code 1.105 of Spanish law, it would not be considered a breach of contract if delays were caused by accidents or Acts of God. In Spanish this would read: *No supondra incumplimiento de los plazos previstos en este contrato los retrasos producidos, por caso fortuito o fuerza mayor de los recogidos en el articulo 1.105 del Codigo Civil.* This would extend the completion date until the unwell person was able to attend the Notary's to sign the *Escritura*, or a Power of Attorney was in place for someone to sign on their behalf. For this clause to be effective there must of course be, in the case of a serious illness, medical proof that this is the reason for invoking this clause and delaying completion.

• The Contract of Purchase & Sale should state who pays the *Plus Valia* **tax** (See Chapter 4 for more details). It should be vendors but agreements vary. Responsibility must be reflected in the *Escritura* deeds.

- If property was built within the last 5 to 6 years, ask for proof that a **building licence was obtained** and that a **certificate of completion of building**, *Certificado de Fin de Obra,* and a licence of first occupation, *Licencia de Primera Ocupacion,* have been issued. If the vendors do not have these, your lawyer can get copies from the Town Hall. You could run into difficulties if these documents have not been obtained and paid for.

Declaring a price

It has been common in Spain to **under-declare a sale price** because of high transfer taxes on resale property – currently totalling 8%. Tax on the sale of new property is currently 4%. An example: a property may be sold for 200,000 Euros, but the price on the *Escritura* deeds maybe shows 150,000 Euros.

The taxman is keenly aware of this and is now a lot stricter. My firm advice would be to **declare the actual price being paid** to avoid potentially high capital gains taxes when you come to sell.

The flipside is that with Spanish property prices having dropped dramatically since 2008, you may honestly declare the actual amount paid, only to find the authorities slap a higher value on the property and tax you accordingly. The way they calculate this varies regionally and with time. In Nerja, where I live, tax authorities set a minimum declared value of 2 times the *Valor Catastral* rateable value in 2004. In 2005, this 'coefficient' was 2.2, rose to 2.7 in 2008, but had fallen to 1.8 in 2012.

The upshot is that **tax can be higher than the sale price would imply**. Bear in mind too that the authorities have four years to check the price you declared. If they value it at a higher price they can issue a *Complimentario,* a supplementary charge, and impose fines too.

Your lawyer can advise on the **minimum value** that the taxman will likely put on the property. In this way you will avoid facing a supplementary charge between 6% and 10% depending on the *Transmisiones Patrimoniales* that apply when you are buying - on the difference between the purchase price declared and the valuation the tax authorities put on it. You also want to avoid fines.

A reminder: be guided by your lawyer on the declared value and this should be agreed with the vendors before signing contracts and paying the deposit.

When you have your NIE certificate (Page 12), you or your lawyer will need to **take photocopies to the Notary's office** where you will sign or have signed your *Escritura,* as the Notary or your lawyer will need the certificates to pay taxes at the Land Registry.

You will also need your NIE certificate to transfer the contract for the electricity and water, to insure the property and of course to pay your annual property taxes in future. These are explained in greater detail in Chapter 12.

Before going to the Notary's to sign the *Escritura,* your lawyer should obtain a **certificate from the *Recaudacion Provincial,*** the local Rates Office, stating that there are no outstanding rates owed on the property. This is presented to the Notary's office when preparing your *Escritura* for signing. The Notary needs the reference number from the certificate to prepare the *Escritura* and obtain a certificate from the Rates Office.

As for **Annual Community Fees**, your lawyer or estate agent should obtain a certificate from the Administrator of the Community showing that fees on the property you are purchasing have been paid up to date. This certificate is then taken up in the Escritura, stating that there are no outstanding community fees.

It has been my normal practice to obtain a *Nota Simple* from the Land Registry on the day of the signing of the *Escritura.* This ensures that no debts or mortgages have been registered on the property since the initial search was made, the contracts were drawn up, and the deposit was paid. This precaution is no longer necessary as the **Notary is obliged to obtain, by fax, a *Nota Simple*** from the Land Registry showing any debts or encumbrances registered against the property. Your lawyer or estate agent should organise this with the Notary at least three days before the signing and at the same time present all the relevant documentation that the notary's office needs to prepare the *Escritura*.

If the property you are buying is being sold in Euros, you would get your Spanish bank (Page 11) to issue **a Banker's Draft** for the final payment. In this case, make sure you allow enough time for funds to be transferred to your Spanish account for the completion.

If the property is foreign-owned, the vendors may want payment in their country's currency, for example in British Pounds or US Dollars. This is perfectly legal. In this case, I suggest you agree an exchange rate against the Euro before signing the *Contrato de CompraVenta* contract of purchase and sale, and have this rate stipulated in the contract. If final payment is being made in one of these currencies, you will need a Banker's Draft from your bank to take to Spain for signing the *Escritura* deeds. The currency website xe.com is one widely used and well regarded source for latest rates.

A Banker's Draft, known as a Cashier's Check in the USA, is a cheque guaranteed by your bank. The funds are removed from your account when the draft is issued, thus ensuring payment to the person or persons to whom the cheque is made payable. In my experience, this is the easiest and safest way to make final payment. Similarly, if you are paying the balance in Euros, you simply ask your Spanish bank to issue a Banker's Draft before going to the Notary to sign the *Escritura* deeds.

Remember! Before handing over the Banker's Draft to the vendors at the Notary, the estate agent or your lawyer should have obtained the **last receipts for electricity, telephone and water** - if the water is not included in the community fees - to ensure that there are no outstanding debts and also to deal with the transfer of these utilities to your name.

When you go to the Notary, you will present your passport/s, your NIE certificate/s and the Banker's Draft/s. The Notary's staff will scan your passport/s into their computer and photocopy the draft/s on to official notarial paper. If the sale is in a different currency, they will still photocopy the drafts on to official notarial paper but will need to know the exchange rate used against the Euro to show the Euro amount on the *Escritura* so that they can calculate transfer taxes etc. Your lawyer or estate agent will no doubt advise you on this matter.

You will recall that if the property is a resale property and the vendors are either **not** Spanish nationals or are foreign nationals **not** fiscally resident in Spain, **you must retain 3% of the sale price** declared on the *Escritura,* which you deduct from the outstanding balance. Or to put it another way, the vendor only gets 97% of the declared price. The 3% withheld must be paid to the local tax authorities within 30 days of signing the *Escritura,* this retention acting as a deposit against the vendor's assumed capital gains tax.

Effectively, you are acting for the tax man to collect some of the vendors' assumed capital gains on the deal. Under normal circumstances your lawyer will deal with paying the retained 3% to the tax authorities on your behalf.

Beware though! If final payment is in British Pounds, for example, you must still transfer funds to Spain to cover payments in Euros of the 3% retention, if that applies, plus Notary and Land Registry fees etc. Transfer such funds at least 10 working days prior to completion date to ensure that they are sent in good time.

Let us assume that you have now signed the *Escritura* deeds and have handed over the Banker's Drafts and are the happy legal owners of your property in Spain. Well done! But there is still a little bit more to deal with.

You must now pay the costs of the *Escritura* and obtain a *Copia Simple,* a simple copy of your *Escritura.* In some cases, the Notary may be able to prepare your *Copia Simple* immediately and let you know the costs, or you or your lawyer may have to return in a few days to collect it and pay the charges.

If these taxes and other fees are not paid within 28 days of signing the *Escritura,* fines for late payment are levied. There is normally a longer period allowed for the *Plus Valia* tax to be paid, but a copy of your *Escritura* must be presented at the local Town Hall **within one month of the signing**. My advice is to avoid any hassle by paying these costs as soon as you know them.

After making the payments, to your lawyer or to the Notary's office, they will take a first copy of the original of your *Escritura* to the Land Registry for them to register the document.

After some two to three months, your *Escritura* will be collected by either your lawyer or the notary's office and you can pick up the first copy of the original. If you are collecting the *Escritura* from the Notary, you present your *Copia Simple* and proof of identity then take away your registered *Escritura.*

Congratulations! You have safely negotiated the Spanish property maze with a little help from your trusted professional advisers. You may even get a nice surprise and receive a small refund from the registration of your *Escritura,* as the amount held by your lawyer or the Notary for the Land Registry is a deposit, and they normally ask for more than is needed to cover this fee.

If you should lose what is classed as 'the original' of your *Escritura,* do not worry. The so-called First Copy of the *Escritura,* minus your signature, goes to the Land Registry and this is what you receive when it is returned to the Notary with all registration details. This document is what is commonly known as 'the original' even if it is not. The Notary retains the true original that you all signed.

Once you have your *Copia Simple* of the *Escritura,* you or your lawyer will need to **take a few photocopies**. These are to:

- pay *Plus Valia* tax at the local Town Hall
- change the *Contribuciones IBI* (annual rates) to your name
- transfer the electricity contract to your name
- transfer the water contract to your name
- give to the administrator of the community of owners

The relevant forms will have to be filled in and signed. This may not be easy for you but, as explained in Chapter 4 on *Escritura Costs*, the agent you are buying the property through, or your lawyer, should make the necessary photocopies for you. They will either go along with you to the various offices, or will do so on your behalf.

Your lawyer or the estate agent that you are buying the property through should go with you to the local office of the electricity company to change the name on the contract. The same applies to water if it is not included in the community fees.

To provide some idea of **fees when transferring the contract** to your name: if it is for the same number of kilowatts (kWs) installed capacity as the previous owner, the cost will be around 26 Euros to 32 Euros. If you want more power, it will cost you 65 Euros for each increase in the number of kWs contracted. So if you want to boost the supply from 2.22 kW to 3.45 kW, the charge would be 65 Euros for bumping up the wattage as well as 26 Euros to 32 Euros to switch it into your name: grand total 91 Euros to 97 Euros. This is an example from Nerja near Málaga. It may be different where you are buying.

Depending on the property's age, you may be obliged by the electricity company to install **a new trip-switch system** and to replace wiring from the trip-switch box to the electricity meter. This must be done by an **approved electrician** who will then obtain a ***Boletin de Instalacion***, a certificate approving the installation. You will not be able to transfer the electricity to you name without this.

The **cost of all this can vary enormously**, but you need to know that it can currently (2012) vary from around 600 Euros to 1,500

Euros depending on the work involved. You, or your lawyer or estate agent, need to present the *Boletin de Instalacion* along with a copy of your *Escritura* and your NIE certificate as well as a copy of the previous owner's electricity bill with the reference number of the electricity meter. It can be an old bill from the vendors, though the last bill they received would be better, because if the estate agent is doing his job properly, when he goes to get the meter reading the day before signing at the notary's he knows how much electricity has been consumed since the last bill and can thus calculate the outstanding amount owed for power.

The electricity company will need a telephone number so they can send an engineer to check the installation and to fit an ICP, a **circuit breaker** to stop you using more kWs than you have contracted for. You will need either to be at home for the engineer or to have left keys with the estate agent. The electricity company is unlikely to specify a precise time. It is usually as vague as 'morning, 'afternoon' or 'evening', and even that can slip.

The **water company also charges to switch a meter** to your name. The fee in Nerja, where I live, is between 125 and 150 Euros, and you leave a deposit of 95 Euros for the meter, a sum that should be returned if you subsequently sell the property. This returned sum should be sent to your bank after you have sold the property.

Both the electricity and water companies will also need your bank account details to set up a standing order for the payment of electricity and water consumed.

Your estate agent or lawyer should also advise the *Administrador de Fincas,* the **administrator of your residential community**, of the change of ownership and go to the *Recaudacion Provincial,* the local rates office, to transfer to your name the **responsibility for paying IBI** , the annual levies on property. I deal with transferring the electricity, water, community and annual rates for clients as I believe it should be part of the service the estate agency offers, or should be part of the work of your lawyer, and that there should be no extra charges. Costs involved in the *Escritura* are explained in Chapter 4.

Chapter 2: New Property or a Plot of Land

THIS chapter deals with buying new property within four categories:

I.   To be built from a developer's plan, i.e. 'off plan'
II. Already under construction
III. Recently completed but never lived in
IV. A plot of land and building your own home

I: Buying off plan

This is quite complicated. Documentation is extensive and even more care is needed than when buying a resale property or one that has been completed. You may decide though that the advantages of having a home built to your own specification – choosing kitchen tiles, what rooms will be where, and so on - outweigh disadvantages. Either way, you would be well advised to use a lawyer, preferably one that comes recommended.

Before paying a deposit and signing a contract, your lawyer will obtain a *Nota Simple* from the Land Registry as proof that the seller is indeed the owner of the land and that there are no mortgages or encumbrances on it. Your lawyer must also see proof that a building licence has been obtained from the local Town Hall, and paid for.

If the property is near the beach, your lawyer should ensure that development is approved by the *Jefatura de Costas.* the Coastal Authority, as well as the *Ayuntamiento,* Town Hall. The *Ley de Costas,* Law of the Coasts, which came into force in 1998, restricts building within 100 metres of the high-tide mark.

If a planning application for the property was submitted to the Town Hall after the May 5, 2000, the developer is obliged to have an insurance policy called *Seguro Decenal,* which guarantees the foundations and structure for 10 years. It does not currently cover the quality of other building materials used, though it is anticipated that these will be included at some later date.

To obtain this insurance policy, an approved and registered company must first carry out a geological survey. Test drillings establish what foundations are required while laboratory analysis is carried out on the quality of the reinforced concrete being used for the foundations and structure.

Without this insurance policy, an *Escritura* deed cannot be obtained for the property, so it is very important. Details of the policy must be included in the contracts for the property.

It makes sense to have some idea of the costs of the *Escritura* before signing and paying a deposit. Your lawyer will be able to give you a breakdown of approximate costs. It should also state who is responsible for paying the *Plus Valia* tax, which should be paid by the seller. This applies to all categories of property in this chapter.

Another important thing to remember when buying from a developer or builder is that they will almost certainly try to persuade you to declare in the *Escritura* a much lower purchase price than you are actually paying.

It has been common practice in Spain to under-declare, but my strong advice is to state the true price.

You will need a bank account (page 11) in Spain to pay the deposit, to make stage payments for the property, and to later pay standing orders for electricity bills, community fees, water, annual rates (IBI).and annual property taxes.

A reminder: **when transferring funds to your Spanish bank**, the details must show it is for the purchase of the property you are buying. It is imperative that all payments are made to the developer or builder by your Spanish bank, because you will need a certificate or certificates from your bank in Spain for the Notary's office, showing that funds to purchase have been imported legally.

So let us assume that **you have chosen the plot, have seen the plans, and that contracts are now being drawn up**. It is vital that all the following details are included in this Contract:

i. The total square metres of the land/plot, the square metres of the house/villa/apartment, and the total price, when the building is completed and ready for you to move into.

ii. The **deposit**, normally 25% of the total price, and the stage payments - normally 25% on completion of the roof; 25% on tiling the bathroom and kitchen and plastering the walls, 25% on the completion of the building, the signing of the *Escritura* and the handing over of keys. As you are initially paying a considerable sum on signing the contracts, and in future stage payments, it is imperative that your lawyer has checked everything thoroughly before signing contracts.

iii. Your bank will release stage payments to the developer or builder only on receipt of an Architects' Certificate, stating that each stage has been completed. If you are not in Spain during building, and will not be around to make stage payments yourself, then you must leave instructions with your Spanish bank to release money only on receipt of these certificates. **I really must stress how important this is.**

iv. The developer or builder is responsible for obtaining the following and payment of the same:

- *Seguro Decenal*: The 10-year insurance policy for foundations and structure.

- *Licencia de Obra*: The Building Licence from the local Town Hall;

- Architect & Surveyor fees for the complete building project for the house/villa/apartment and when the building is completed;

- *Certificado de Fin de Obra* and the *Licencia de Primera Ocupacion*: These are the Certificate of Building Completion and the Licence of First Occupation.

- *Boletin de Instalacion*: The Certificate of Installation issued by the *Delegacion de Industria* (Delegation of Industry) for electricity and water. You need copies to obtain the electric and water meters.

v. All **registration details** of the land where your property is being built must be included: the *Finca* No. (The registered land number at the Land Registry), the Book No., and so on. Your lawyer should extract this information from either the *Escritura* of the land/plot or the *Nota Simple* (The Registration Document from the Land Registry).

vi. A detailed plan of the property showing the square metres, the specifications of the building and, where applicable, prices per square metre of floor and wall tiles. A very detailed specification of the building and installations is required to ensure that no hidden extras appear during construction. The plans and specification should be annexed to the Contracts and signed by all parties. In Spanish, this is called a *Memoria de Calidades*.

vii. If a **kitchen is being installed**, then a detailed plan must be prepared showing exactly what is being fitted and what domestic appliances are included. It should also make clear that taps and plumbing connections are included. This should also be annexed to the Contract and signed by all parties.

viii. If you are having a gas cooker or hob, or the water heating is gas fired, the **gas installation** should be included. The inspection and contract for the gas supply, and payment, which is the responsibility of the developer or builder, should also be reflected either in the Contract or specification. If there is no mains gas and you have to have gas cylinders, as is often the case in small towns or villages, the developer or builder must supply you with the contract to obtain gas cylinders.

ix. The developer or builder is responsible for obtaining and paying for the **certificates for installation** of the electricity and water so that you can have meters installed. You should be responsible only for payment for the installation of electricity and water meters.

x. If the **garden is being landscaped**, as is the norm in Spain, this should also be specified in the Contract or the building specification.

xi. It should be clearly specified in the Contract what your '**quota of participation**' in the Community of Owners will be. If the Community has not yet been formed, at least you will know what percentage you will have to pay towards the fees. If the Community has already been formed, ask what your fees will be, as these can often be anything up to 2,000 Euros or more annually depending on services and facilities included.

xii. The developer or builder is responsible for the payment of all **debts on the land**, i.e. *IBI* (Annual Rates) and any other charges up until the time that you take possession of the property.

xiii. A **penalty clause** will doubtless be included in the Contract to the effect that if you fail to meet the payments agreed, the contract becomes null and void and you not only lose the amounts already paid but the developer or builder will be free to offer your property for sale to another party. So, as in buying a resale property (Chapter 1), you must be sure that you will be able to meet these payments when they become due.

xiv. A further penalty clause should be included in the Contract to state that if the building is not completed on the date agreed, then the developer or builder must pay an **indemnity for each day after the completion date**. The sum per day must be negotiated with the developer or builder and reflected in the Contract. It should be enough to cover, for example, the cost of a daily rate for you and your family to stay in a hotel until such time as the building is completed. As you can see, if you proceed in the correct way with a property purchase, you are well protected should anything go slightly awry!

xv. The **final payment and the signing of the *Escritura*** will be made on completion of the building and presentation of the

Certificate of the Termination of the Building *(Certificado de Fin de Obra)* and the *Licencia de Primera Ocupacion* (Licence of First Occupation).

xvi. It should be made clear in the Contract that you are **responsible only for the payment of the costs of the *Escritura* for the sale and purchase of the property**, not the segregation of your plot from the rest of the land *(Segregacion)*, the declaration of a new building *(Declaracion de Obra Nueva)*, or the Horizontal Division *(Division Horizontal)* in the case of an apartment. The costs of the *Segregacion* (segregating your plot from the rest of the *Urbanizacion)*, the *Declaracion de Obra Nueva* (Declaring the new building) and, in the case of an apartment, the *Division Horizontal* (Horizontal Division) are the responsibility of the developer or builder. It should also state who is responsible for the payment of the *Plus Valia* tax. This should be paid by the seller (See Chapter 4 for more details of this tax) and of course must be reflected in the *Escritura* when you go to sign at the Notary's office.

xvii. Your lawyer should check to see if the land is **registered for Annual Rates** (IBI) If so, your lawyer must obtain a certificate to show that the IBI has been paid up to date. Once the property is completed, the building must also be registered with the rates office *(Recaudacion Provincial): see* Pages 35/36 for more details.

If you request any **alterations or additions to the property** under construction, you must always ask for a **written quotation**, and this should be signed by both parties, to save any disputes on 'extras' when the building is completed. Any major alterations or additions may also extend the completion date of the building. If this is the case, a new completion date should be agreed in writing and signed by both parties, as this will obviously affect the penalty clause for late completion in the Contract.

The following applies to all purchases in this chapter.

You must obtain an NIE (Page 12). When you have your NIE certificate, you or your lawyer must take photocopies to the Notary's office when you go to sign your *Escritura* title deed for the property. This is because either the Notary or your lawyer will need these to pay taxes at the Land Registry. Fines for late payment will be levied if these taxes and other fees are not paid within 28 days of the *Escritura* signing,

A longer period is usually allowed to pay the *Plus Valia* tax, but a copy of your *Escritura* must be presented at the *Ayuntamiento*, Town Hall, within one month of the signing. My advice is to pay these costs as soon as you know them. Note that the IVA (Spanish value added tax) of the declared purchase price on the *Escritura* must be paid to the developer before the *Escritura* is signed, and the fact that you have paid the IVA must be reflected in the *Escritura*.

You also need your NIE to insure the property, for the installation of the electricity meter, the water meter, and in future to pay the annual taxes on the property. These are fully explained in Chapter 12.

So you have now signed the *Escritura*, have handed over final payment, and are now the happy legal owners of your property in Spain. Well done! But there is still a little bit more to deal with.

You must now pay the costs of the *Escritura* and obtain a *Copia Simple*, a simple copy of your *Escritura*. In some cases, the Notary may be able to prepare your *Copia Simple* immediately and let you know the costs, or you or your lawyer may have to return in a few days to collect it and pay the charges involved.

If these taxes and other fees are not paid within 28 days of the signing of the *Escritura*, fines for late payment will be levied. There is normally a longer period allowed for the *Plus Valia* tax to be paid, but a copy of your *Escritura* must be presented at the local Town Hall (*Ayuntamiento*) within one month of the signing. My advice is to avoid any hassle by paying these costs as soon as you know how much you have to pay.

After making the payments, to your lawyer or to the Notary's office, they will take a first copy of the original of your *Escritura* to the Land Registry for them to register the document. After some two to three months, your *Escritura* will be collected by either your lawyer or the notary's office and you can pick up the first copy of the original.

If collecting the *Escritura* from the Notary, you present your *Copia Simple* and proof of identity then take away your registered *Escritura* .Congratulations! You have safely negotiated the Spanish property maze with a little help from your trusted professional advisers. You may even get a nice surprise and receive a small refund from the registration of your *Escritura,* as the amount held by your lawyer or the Notary for the Land Registry is a deposit and they normally ask for more than is needed to cover this fee.

If by any chance you should lose what is classed as 'the original' of your *Escritura,* it is not a disaster for reasons already explained earlier.

Once you have a *Copia Simple* of your *Escritura,* your lawyer will need to take a few photocopies. These are to:

- Register for the *Plus Valia* tax at the Town Hall
- Register the IBI *Contribuciones,* annual property rates, in your name.
- To contract the electricity meter.
- Obtain a water meter if not already installed by the Developer/Builder.

The relevant forms will have to be filled in and signed. This may not be easy for you but, remember that the estate agent that you are buying the property through, or your lawyer, should make the necessary photocopies for you and either go with you to the various offices or do so on your behalf. Costs involved in obtaining the *Escritura* are explained in Chapter 4.

Note well: All the documents mentioned are crucial. Without the *Certificado de Fin de Obra,* Building Completion Certificate, the *Licencia de Primera Ocupacion,* Licence of First Occupation, and the *Seguro Decenal* to prove that there is a 10-yera insurance policy for the building, you will be unable to sign the *Escritura* title deeds at the Notary's office. Nor will you be able to get an electricity or water meter, which means no electricity or water supply.

The *Fin de Obra,* Building Completion Certificate, is issued by the architect and a copy is presented to the Planning Department of the local Town Hall. This document informs the authorities that the building has been finished in accordance with plans presented when the original application was made.
The Planning Department then sends an Inspector to measure the building to see if it matches these plans and, all being well, they then issue the *Licencia de Primera Ocupacion,* Licence of First Occupation.

If the property has *not* been built in accordance with the plans submitted to the planning department, they will *not* issue the *Licencia de Primera Ocupacion,* Licence of First Occupation. Hence the importance of obtaining this document from the Developer/Builder before making the final payment and signing the *Escritura* title deeds.

You should also receive a copy of the *Certificado de Fin de Obra,* Building Completion Certificate, which is supplied by the architect, and the original of the *Licencia de Primera Ocupacion,* the Licence of First Occupation.

When buying a new property being built for you, it is very important when the building is completed that the Developer/ Builder **registers your property** with the *Recaudacion Provincial,* the local Rates Office. This is also something that could be included in the Contract, so that the Developer/Builder commits to do this on completion of the building. Indeed, many Town Halls in Spain and her islands will not issue the *Licencia de Primera Ocupacion,* the Licence of First Occupation, without seeing proof that the property built has been registered with the *Recaudacion Provincial.* Of course without the *Licencia de Primera Ocupacion,* you will neither be able to sign the *Escritura* title deeds nor obtain your electricity or water meters.

II: **A property already under construction**

Buying unfinished property is less complicated than having it built from plans, but there can be pitfalls. Before a contract is drawn up and signed, your lawyer should see proof that the Developer/Builder is the legal owner of the land, so should ask to see a copy of the *Escritura* and a *Nota Simple* as proof of ownership and validation that there are no encumbrances on the land.

Let us assume that **your desired house, villa or apartment is already constructed to roof level.** What should be in the Contract?

i.   As when purchasing off-plan property from a developer/builder, they must have obtained and paid for the *Licencia de Obra,* Building Licence, from the local *Ayuntamiento,* Town Hall. The details of the building licence must be reflected in the *Contrato de CompraVenta* contract of purchase and sale. The developer/builder should also have obtained and paid for the *Seguro Decenal,* 10-year insurance policy, if this applies (see bullet point ii below). On completion of the building, the builder/developer is responsible for the obtaining and paying for: the *Certificado de Fin de Obra,* Building Completion Certificate, which is supplied by the Architect; the *Licencia de Primerea Ocupacion,* Licence of First Occupation, issued by the local Town

Hall; and the *Boletin de Instalacion,* Certificate of Installation, issued by the *Delegacion de Industria,* Industry Delegation, for the electricity and water installations. You will need copies of these *Boletins* as well as a copy of the *Licencia de Primera Ocupacion,* Licence of First Occupation, to get your electricity and water meters.

ii. If the planning application for building was presented at the Town Hall after May 5, 2000, the builder/developer must by law have a *Seguro Decenal* ten year insurance policy for the property under construction to guarantee the foundations and structure for that period. It does not currently cover the quality of other building materials used, although it is anticipated that these will be included at some later date. To obtain the insurance policy, an approved and registered company must carry out a geological survey of the land. Test drillings are taken to study the type of foundations required and laboratory tests are carried out on the quality of the reinforced concrete used for the foundations and structure. If the builder/developer does not have this insurance policy, you cannot obtain the *Escritura* title deeds for the property. So it is very important that the details of this policy are reflected in the contracts.

iii. The total square meters of the land/plot and the total constructed area of the property as well as its terraces.

iv. The full registration details of the land/plot, for example the *Finca* number, which is the registration number of the land/plot, the book number etc. This is obtained from either the *Escritura* or the *Nota Simple,* the copy of the Land Registry document.

v. The price for the property should be clearly stated and the payment structure shown in detail. Under normal circumstances, it is possible that as the building is technically already half-built, the Developer/Builder may well ask for 50% as a deposit, with the balance being paid on completion of the building, handing over of the keys and the corresponding *Escritura.*

vi. A detailed plan of the property showing the square metres, specification, and with prices per square metre of floor and wall tiles if applicable. A highly detailed specification of the building and installations is required specifically to ensure that no hidden extras appear during construction. The plans and specification should be annexed to the Contracts and signed by all parties. In Spanish, this is called a *Memoria de Calidades*

vii. If a kitchen is being installed, then a detailed plan should show what is being fitted and what domestic appliances are included. It should also be made clear that taps and plumbing connections are included. This should also be annexed to the Contract and signed by all parties.

viii. If you are having a gas cooker or hob, or the water heating is gas-fired, then the gas installation should be included. The inspection and the contract for the gas supply, payment for which is the responsibility of the Developer/Builder, should also be reflected either in the Contract or specification. If there is no Town Gas and you have to have gas cylinders, as is often the case in small towns or villages, the developer/builder must supply you with the contract to obtain the gas cylinders.

ix. Electricity, water and sewerage is connected to the property and there are no connection charges. You should only pay for the installation of the electricity and water meters and gas cylinders.

x. If the garden is being landscaped, this should also be reflected in the Contract or specification.

xi. Your quota of participation in the Community of Owners should be clearly specified in the Contract.

xii. There will doubtless be a **penalty clause** that if you do not meet payments as specified, the Contract becomes null and void and you lose whatever you have already paid, leaving the Developer/Builder free to offer the property for sale again. So you must be sure before you sign the Contract that you will be able to make payments as agreed.

xiii. A penalty clause should be included stating that if the building is not completed on the agreed date, then the Developer/Builder should pay you as an indemnity a fixed sum for each day after the completion date. It should be enough to cover your expenses to stay in a hotel until the building is completed.

xiv. The final payment and the signing of the *Escritura* will be made on completion of the building and presentation of the *Certificado de Fin de Obra*, Building Completion Certificate, and the *Licencia de Primera Ocupacion*, Licence of First Occupation.

xv. When the *Escritura* title deed is drawn up, you should be responsible only for the costs for the *CompraVenta*, Sale & Purchase, and not the Declaration of the new building, or the *Segregacion de la Finca*, segregation of the land, or the *Division Horizontal*, horizontal division, in the case of an apartment. This should also be clearly stated in the Contract. It should also state who is responsible for the payment of the *Plus Valia* tax. This should be paid by the Vendor (see Chapter 4) and must be reflected in the *Escritura* title deed when you go to sign at the Notary's.

xvi. The Developer/Builder is responsible for all debts on the property until the handing over of the keys and signing of the *Escritura*.

Remember that it is a good idea to ascertain what the approximate costs of the *Escritura* will be before signing the contracts and paying the deposit. This ensures that you do not get a nasty surprise when you go to pay for it at the Notary's office on completion. So ask your lawyer to give you an approximate breakdown of these costs.

You will need a bank account (page 11) in Spain to pay for property if it is being sold in Euros and then to pay standing orders for electricity, community fees, water and rates (IBI).

When transferring funds to your Spanish bank, the documentation must show that it is for the purchase of the property that you are buying. It is imperative that all payments are made to the Developer/Builder by your Spanish bank, because you will need one or more certificates from this bank to show the Notary's office that the funds for the purchase have been imported legally from a foreign country.

If you request **any alterations or additions to the property under construction**, you must always ask for a **written quotation**, and this should be signed by both parties, to save any disputes on 'extras' when the building is completed. Any major alterations or additions may also extend the completion date. If so, a new completion date should be agreed in writing and signed by both parties, as this will obviously affect the penalty clause for late completion in the Contract.

Note well: All the documents mentioned are crucial. Without the *Certificado de Fin de Obra*, Building Completion Certificate, the *Licencia de Primera Ocupacion*, Licence of First Occupation, and the *Seguro Decenal* to prove that there is a 10 Year insurance policy for the building, you will be unable to sign the *Escritura* title deeds at the Notary's office. Nor will you be able to get an electricity or water meter, which means no electricity or water supply.

The *Fin de Obra*, Building Completion Certificate, is issued by the architect and a copy is presented to the Planning Department of the local Town Hall. This document informs the authorities that the building has been finished in accordance with plans presented when the original application was made.

The Planning Department then sends an Inspector to measure the building to see if it matches these plans and, all being well, they then issue the *Licencia de Primera Ocupacion,* Licence of First Occupation. If the property has *not* been built in accordance with the plans submitted to the planning department, they will *not* issue the *Licencia de Primera Ocupacion,* Licence of First Occupation. Hence the importance of obtaining this document from the Developer/Builder before making the final payment and signing the *Escritura* title deeds.

You should also receive a copy of the *Certificado de Fin de Obra,* Building Completion Certificate, which is supplied by the architect, and the original of the *Licencia de Primera Ocupacion,* the Licence of First Occupation.

It should be clearly stated in the Contract that the Developer/Builder is not only responsible for obtaining these documents, but also for their payment.

When buying a new property under construction, it is vital that the Developer/Builder registers the new building with the *Recaudacion Provincial,* the Rates Office. This responsibility should be reflected in the Contract as many Town Halls in Spain and her islands will not issue the *Licencia de Primera Ocupacion,* Licence of First Occupation, without first seeing proof that the property has been registered. Without the *Licencia de Primera Ocupacion,* you will be unable either to sign the *Escritura* title deed or to obtain your electricity or water meter.

III: Property recently completed, but never lived in

Buying a new property, already built but as yet uninhabited, is the least complicated of the options in this chapter. Still, before signing contracts and paying a deposit, your estate agent or lawyer should request a *Nota Simple* from the Land Registry showing that the developer/builder is the registered owner of the land built on, and that it is free of encumbrances. The *Contrato de CompraVenta* contract of purchase and sale must show:

i.   A building licence has been issued and paid for. Details of planning approval should be included.

ii.   If a planning application was submitted after May 5, 2000, the developer must have *Seguro Decenal* insurance guaranteeing foundations and structure for 10-years (Page 46). Without this, an *Escritura* title deed cannot be obtained.

iii.   The certificates, from the Architect and the Town Hall have been obtained, the *Certificado de fin de Obra,* Building Completion Certificate, the *Licencia de Primera Ocupacion,* Licence of First Occupation, and the *Boletin de Instalacion,* Installation Certificate, issued by the *Delegacion de Industria,* Industry Delegation, for the installation of the electricity and water. You need copies of these *Boletins* to get your electricity and water meters. The fact that the Developer/Builder has these documents, and that they have been paid for, should be reflected in the Contract.

iv.   All the registration details must be included: the *Finca* number (the plot/land registration no.), the book number, and so on. This information can be obtained from the *Escritura* title deed or the *Nota Simple* registration document from the Land Registry.

v.   The total square metres of the plot/land and the total constructed area of the property and its terraces should also be included.

vi.   There are no connection charges for electricity, water or sewerage, and that you are responsible only for the payment of the installation of the electric meter and the water meter if they are not already installed. The Developer/Builder should also supply you with the Gas Contract to obtain gas cylinders if gas appliances are installed but there is no piped gas available.

vii.   Your quota of participation in the Community of Owners is clearly stated.

viii. The Developer/Builder is responsible for all debts on the property up to the date of the signing of the *Escritura* and the handing over of the keys.

ix. The price and payments to be made are clearly stated in the Contract.

x. There will likely be a **penalty clause** so that if you do not meet the payments as specified, the Contract becomes null and void and you lose whatever you have already paid, leaving the Developer/Builder free to offer the property for sale again. So you must be sure, before you sign the Contract, that you will be able to make the payment as agreed.

xi. When the *Escritura* title deed is drawn up, you should be responsible only for the costs for the *CompraVenta* contract of purchase and sale, and not for the Declaration of a New Building, or the *Segregacion de la Finca,* segregation of the land, or the *Division Horizontal,* horizontal division, in the case of an apartment. This should be clearly stated in the Contract as should responsibility for the payment of the *Plus Valia* tax, which should be paid by the Vendor (please refer to Chapter 4*)* and be reflected in the *Escritura* when you go to sign at the Notary's.

xii. The final payment and the signing of the *Escritura* will be made on presentation of the *Licencia de Primera Ocupacion,* the Licence of First Occupation.

xiii. Before you sign the Contract, your lawyer must have obtained a *Nota Simple* from the Land Registry proving that the person you are buying the property from is the registered legal owner and that there are no mortgages or encumbrances on the property.

xiv.   Again, before signing the Contract and paying the deposit, it makes sense to have some idea of the costs of the *Escritura.* Your lawyer will be able to give you a breakdown of the approximate costs, to ensure that you do not get a nasty surprise when you go to pay for it at the Notary's office on completion. It should also state who is responsible for the payment of the *Plus Valia* tax, which should be paid by the Vendor.

xv.   You must ask to see proof that the annual *Contribuciones* rates and the community fees are paid up to date, if the community has already been formed, before making the final payment and signing the *Escritura.*

You will need a bank account (Page 11) in Spain to pay for property if it is being sold in Euros and then to pay standing orders for electricity, community fees, water and IBI property rates.

When transferring funds to your Spanish bank, the documentation must show that it is for the purchase of the property that you are buying. It is imperative that all payments are made to the Developer/Builder by your Spanish bank, because you will need one or more certificates from this bank to show the Notary's office that the funds for the purchase have been imported legally from a foreign country.

Note well: All the documents mentioned are crucial. Without the *Certificado de Fin de Obra,* Building Completion Certificate, the *Licencia de Primera Ocupacion,* Licence of First Occupation, and the *Seguro Decenal* (Page 46) to prove that there is a 10 Year insurance policy for the building, you will be unable to sign the *Escritura* title deeds at the Notary's office. Nor will you be able to get an electricity or water meter, which means no electricity or water supply.

The *Fin de Obra,* Building Completion Certificate, is issued by the architect and a copy is presented to the Planning Department of the local Town Hall. This document informs the authorities that the building has been finished in accordance with plans presented when the original application was made.

The Planning Department then sends an Inspector to measure the building to see if it matches these plans and, all being well, they then issue the *Licencia de Primera Ocupacion,* Licence of First Occupation.

If the property has *not* been built in accordance with the plans submitted to the planning department, they will *not* issue the *Licencia de Primera Ocupacion,* Licence of First Occupation. Hence the importance of obtaining this document from the Developer/Builder before making the final payment and signing the *Escritura* title deeds.

You should also receive a copy of the *Certificado de Fin de Obra,* Building Completion Certificate from the architect and the original *Licencia de Primera Ocupacion,* the Licence of First Occupation. Remember that it should be clearly stated in the Contract that the Developer/Builder is not only responsible for obtaining these documents, but also for their payment.

When buying a newly completed property, it is vital that the Developer/Builder registers the new building with the *Recaudacion Provincial* Rates Office. This responsibility should be reflected in the Contract as many Town Halls will not issue the *Licencia de Primera Ocupacion,* Licence of First Occupation, without first seeing proof that the property has been registered. Without the *Licencia de Primera Ocupacion* you will be unable either to sign the *Escritura* title deed or to obtain your electricity or water meter.

IV Buying land then building your own property

If you are thinking of buying land to build your own home, tread very carefully. **Use a lawyer** because the process is fraught with danger.

First, you must ensure that the local *Ayuntamiento,* Town Hall, will give **planning permission** and how many **square metres** they will allow you to build.

The agent or person with whom you are negotiating to buy land may, often in all good faith, say you can build a three or four bedroom villa with a double garage. Then the Town Hall says you can build only a small, two bedroom house with no garage, or you cannot build at all because the land is zoned for agricultural use only, or is not large enough.

To avoid costly disappointment, you or your lawyer should obtain a document called an *Informe Urbanistica* from the Town Hall, and the same document from the *Junta*, the regional government, as a safeguard. This tells exactly what the planners will authorise you to build, the total square metres you can construct, and the maximum height of the building.

So if you really can build your dream home, you now need an **architect and a builder** with good reputations. Finding an architect is easy, and he or she will doubtless help you deal with planning approval.

For some idea of fees, I asked a local architect for a ballpark figure for a property of 120 square metres. He estimated a total cost, including surveyor's fees, in the region of 5,500 Euros including value added tax.

The estimate of building costs is presented to the Town Hall by your architect along with the project details. The Town Hall uses the estimated build cost to levy a charge for a building licence. In 2012, the Town Hall where I live was charging 7.6% of the figure quoted by the Architect for the cost of building. This will likely vary from one town to another, so use this purely as a guide.

On top of these costs, you are legally obliged to have a *Seguro Decenal* **insurance policy** guaranteeing the quality of the foundations and structure of the property for 10 years. This insurance does not currently cover the quality of other building materials used, though it is anticipated that these will be included at some later date. If the builder does not have this insurance policy, you cannot obtain the *Escritura* title deeds for the property.

In our example, the cost of this policy for our 120 square metre property would be around 7,900 Euros. You must use an insurance agency specialising in *Seguro Decenal*. Your architect will likely contact an appropriate agency and give you a quotation for costs.

But beware! When paying the architect for the project/plans, you will normally pay only 70% of the total cost initially. The remaining 30% falls due for payment when the building is finished. Unfortunately, when people receive the first account from the architect, they often think they have paid the fees in full.

Once the building is completed, the architect issues a *Certificado de Fin de Obra*, a Building Completion Certificate, and presents it to the *Ayuntamiento* on your behalf.

The Town Hall inspects the property to check that it has been built in accordance with the plans presented. If all is in order, they issue the *Licencia de Primera Ocupacion*, Licence of First Occupation which you need this to make the *Declaracion de Obra Nueva,* declaration of a new building, at the Notary's office.

You simply must find a good builder, which is not always easy. There are 'cowboy' builders in every country, but just imagine how much more difficult it is going to be in a foreign place.

Ask people who already live in your target area if they know of a good builder: there is nothing like personal recommendations.

Once you have found a builder, your lawyer should draw up a complete specification for the building work reflecting, for example, the cost per square metre for tiles, the models and types of sanitary fittings, taps, doors, windows etc. A completion date should be fixed, with a penalty clause for late completion (See point x. on page 43).

This document is a contract and should be signed by all concerned.

If you still want to build a property, be aware that the **cost may be much greater than first imagined**, even when buying from a Developer/Builder, as there are always extras that you want as work progresses. If you request any alterations or additions, ask for a written quotation. This should be signed by both parties to prevent disputes on building completion.

Major alterations or additions may also extend completion. If so, a new date should be agreed in writing and signed by both parties, as this will affect the **penalty clause for late completion** in the Contract.

Spend as much time as possible on site when your property is being built. This is to ensure that everything is in accordance with the plans and also to be on hand to request changes, such as having an arch rather than a square opening between rooms. You may choose tiles, or may tell the electrician where you want sockets or wall lights.

If you are on site, things can be dealt with on the spot rather than receiving phone calls or e-mails which can slow things considerably.

When building on your own land, the electrician and plumber must obtain a *Boletin de Instalacion*, Certificate of Installation, from the *Delegacion de Industria*, Industry Delegation, approving the installation, as you will need these certificates to get your electricity and water meters. These certificates can be obtained only by registered electricians and plumbers who must be members of the *Asociacion Provincial de Instaladores*.

You must pay for the land via your Spanish bank account, as you will need a certificate from the bank proving that the funds have been imported legally from your country of origin.

Payments to the builder must also be made through a Spanish Bank account and registered clearly as payments for the building of your villa. This is most important as you will also need a certificate/s from your Spanish bank showing that the funds were imported into Spain to pay your builder. You will need these certificates for the Notary when you go to sign for the land that you are buying and later on when you go back to make the *Declaracion de Obra Nueva*, Declaration of a New Building, on your land.

You must also **register the new building** with the *Recaudacion Provincial*, the Rates Office, which is normally in the capital of the province that you are buying in. Your lawyer or architect should be able to deal with this for you.

Registering your property with the Rates Office is vital because many Town Halls in Spain will not issue the *Licencia de Primera Ocupacion*, Licence of First Occupation, without first seeing proof that the new building has been registered with the *Recaudacion Provincial*. Without the Licence of First Occupation you will be unable to declare the new building at the Notary's.

If you do go ahead and buy land and a Contract is drawn up for the purchase of it, you should follow pretty much the instructions given in Chapter I, dealing with buying a resale property, with regard to the documentation required and what should be included in the Contract.

If you are buying land and building a property, then you will technically be making two *Escrituras*. When you pay the balance owing for the land, you will make the *Escritura* for the land and will later return to the Notary's to declare the new building on your land once the property is completed. Please refer to Chapter 4 for fuller details of these costs.

Chapter 3 Rural and Inherited Property

HERE we deal with buying a *finca,* farmland, **cortijo,** farm-house, or a house in a **pueblo,** Spanish village. If the *finca* or village house is very old and has been handed down through generations, there may be no *Escritura* title deed for it. You must tread very carefully and will definitely need the help of a Spanish lawyer.

Remove those rose-tinted spectacles when looking at farm properties. Living there may not be as idyllic as it first appears. In hilly and mountainous areas, such properties are up dirt tracks, very often a considerable distance from a tarmac road. When the rain comes in the winter – often as torrential, tropical type storms - tracks can become almost impassable and you would almost certainly need a four-wheel drive vehicle (4WD) to get to and from the property.

There is often no electricity supply and connecting one can be very expensive, even if it is possible. Shops and facilities are not on your doorstep, and what if someone is taken ill? Think country by all means, but think carefully.

There are legal restrictions on whether you can build or extend properties on a *finca,* farmland, depending on what use the land is classified for and on size.

Rustica/Regadio is rustic land not programmed for development, or farmland with trees and a water supply, and you will normally need a minimum of 10,000 square metres. *Secano,* dry land, usually needs to be a minimum of 30,000 square metres.

The catch is that the size required for building in both these categories can vary tremendously from one area of Spain to another, so you must get your lawyer to check before signing contracts and handing over a deposit.

If there is no building on the *finca* land and you plan a new house, your lawyer must obtain an *Informe Urbanistica* from the *Ayuntamiento,* Town Hall, to see what, if anything, you may be authorised to build:

notably the total square metres that you might build and if you would be allowed more than one storey.

Your Lawyer/Architect must also establish if authorisation is needed from the **regional government** offices, often known as the *Junta,* allowing you to build on this land.

Some regional governments are now overruling local Town Halls that have authorised building in rural areas. In some cases, these *Juntas* are banning building regardless of the square meterage of the land. So your Lawyer/Architect must get authorisation from both *Junta* and *Ayuntamiento* before you go ahead with the purchase and pay deposits.

If there is a *cortijo,* farmhouse, on land that you are buying and you wish to alter or extend existing property, or to demolish it and build a new house, you must get your Lawyer/Architect to obtain the same information - an *Informe Urbanistica* and possibly authorisation from the *Junta* - as you may not be able to extend the existing structure but only renovate what is already there.

You may not be able to demolish the existing building and build a new house. If you *can* demolish the existing property, you may only be allowed to rebuild the same number of square metres that were already built.

You will of course need planning permission to extend or demolish the existing property and build a new house, which means you will need plans drawn up by an architect and you are legally obliged to obtain a *Seguro Decenal* insurance policy (Page 46). For more details on this refer to Chapter 2.

Remember, you must use the services of a recommended lawyer when buying one of these types of property. He or she should be consulted before signing any contracts and handing over any deposits.

If the property you are buying is Spanish-owned, or the sellers are foreign but have *residencia,* residency status, and can prove that they are fiscally resident in Spain, then payments to them must be made through your Spanish bank account. This is because you will need certificates for the Notary proving that the funds for the purchase have been imported legally into Spain from a foreign country.

It is vital to reflect the **exact square metres** of the *finca* in the Contract of Purchase & Sale. I know cases where purchasers were told there were 5,000 square metres, which was not reflected in the contract, only to discover when the *Escritura* was signed that there were only 1,500.

Equally, the square metres, the number of bedrooms, and other relevant details, should be checked against the *Escritura* title deed as the present owners may have extended the property without declaring the new building at the Notary's Office.

If this is the case and they have had planning permission from the local Town Hall and have a *Declaracion de Fin de Obra* and a *Licencia de Primera Ocupacion*, they must make a *Declaracion de Obra Nueva*, Declaration of a New Building, at the Notary's before you buy.

If planning permission has not been granted for extensions, your lawyer needs to know if it can and what the costs would be, which of course should be paid by the present owners. Your lawyer should advise you on this.

Rights of Way

It is important to have rights of way and water rights included in the *Escritura* title deed: water is normally supplied from a shared well in the countryside. I recommend that you ask your lawyer to get a certificate, the *Certificado Descriptivo y Grafico con Linderos* from the *Catastral* offices, which are normally in the main city of the province where the property is situated.

This plan of the land shows the boundaries, exact square metres, and the square metres constructed. Your lawyer can download this online and should produce it along with all other documentation at the Notary's office when you sign the *Escritura* title deed. He should also contact the owner of the well to find out how much water has been contracted for.

With these plans, you could then have a topographical survey made to clearly mark the boundaries of your land. When you are being shown land, it is quite customary for the owner or whoever is showing it to you, to tell you that the boundary is such and such an olive tree. Or they might pick up a stone and throw it, saying that where it falls is roughly where the boundary is. This makes for a colourful anecdote to tell your friends, but having clearly marked boundary and plans could prevent future disputes erupting. It always makes good sense to be prepared.

You will need a bank account in Spain to pay if the vendor is selling in Euros and then to pay standing orders for electricity, community fees, water and rates (IBI). See Page 11

A longer period is usually allowed to pay the *Plus Valia* tax, but a copy of your *Escritura* must be presented at the *Ayuntamiento*, Town Hall, within one month of the signing. My advice is to pay these costs as soon as you know them.

You will also need a copy of your NIE certificate for the Notary, when you go to sign the *Escritura*, to insure the property, the transfer the electricity meter, the water meter, and in future to pay the annual taxes on the property. These are fully explained in Chapter 12.

So you have now signed the *Escritura*, have handed over final payment, and are now the happy legal owners of your land/house in Spain. Well done! But there is still a little bit more to deal with.

You must now pay the costs of the *Escritura* and obtain a *Copia Simple*, a simple copy of your *Escritura*. In some cases, the Notary may be able to prepare your *Copia Simple* immediately and let you know the costs, or you or your lawyer may have to return in a few days to collect it and pay the charges involved.

If these taxes and other fees are not paid within 28 days of the signing of the *Escritura*, fines for late payment will be levied. There is normally a longer period allowed for the *Plus Valia* tax to be paid, but a copy of your *Escritura* must be presented at the local Town Hall (*Ayuntamiento*) within one month of the signing. My advice is to avoid any hassle by paying these costs as soon as you know how much you have to pay.

After making the payments, to your lawyer or to the Notary's office, they will take a first copy of the original of your *Escritura* to the Land Registry for them to register the document.

After some two to three months, your *Escritura* will be collected by either your lawyer or the notary's office and you can pick up the first copy of the original. If collecting the *Escritura* from the Notary, you present your *Copia Simple* and proof of identity then take away your registered *Escritura.* Congratulations!

You may even get a small refund from the registration of your *Escritura,* as the amount held by your lawyer or the Notary for the Land Registry is a deposit and they normally ask for more than is needed to cover this fee.

If by any chance you should lose what is classed as 'the original' of your *Escritura,* it is not a disaster. As you have learned, the so-called First Copy of the *Escritura,* minus your signature, is sent to the Land Registry and this is what you receive when it is returned to the Notary's with all the registration details. This document is what is commonly known as 'the original' even if it is not really that. Happily, the Notary retains the true original that you all signed.

Once you have a *Copia Simple* of your *Escritura,* your lawyer will need to take a few photocopies. These are to: **register for the *Plus Valia*** tax at the Town Hall; **register the IBI *Contribuciones***, annual rates/Council Tax, in your name; **transfer the electric meter** to your name; and to **transfer the water meter** to your name if your water is supplied by the local water board.

If there is **no title deed**, a lawyer may be able to obtain an ***Expediente de Dominio,*** Proof of Domination, a document proving ownership and issued by the Courts. A search is made to prove ownership and a notice is then put in the *Boletin Oficial del Estado,* an official state paper, to give anyone with claims on the property the chance to come forward.

It can take considerable time to obtain an *Expediente de Dominio,* from a year to 18 months and possibly longer. Your lawyer will retain a reasonable sum from the agreed price until this document is available but this applies only when he or she is satisfied that the vendor can show sufficient proof of ownership and can register the property at the Land Registry. Once you have the *Expediente de Dominio,* it is the same as having an *Escritura* title deed.

It may be suggested that you use a Tax Form 205 procedure to obtain the *Escritura* for the property. You can obtain an *Escritura* in a much shorter period of time with this document than with the *Expediente de Dominio.* The drawback of the Tax Form 205 strategy is that for a period of two years from the date that your *Escritura* is registered at the Land Registry, somebody could claim ownership of the property.

This is probably very unlikely to happen, as your lawyer would have checked all relevant documents from the present owners, proving ownership, and would have checked with the Land Registry to get a document called a *Certificado Negativo,* a Negative Certificate showing that a records search had found no registered owner of the property.

However, it is a remote possibility that someone may come forward, and you should at least be aware of it. Your lawyer should explain both formats, the *Expediente de Dominio* and the 205, and advise on the best way to obtain an *Escritura* for the property. Be aware that you will not be able to get a mortgage until such time as an *Escritura* is registered either through the 205 Tax Form or the *Expediente de Dominio* at the Land Registry.

If the property you are buying has been inherited and the deceased owner had a Will & Testament leaving it to the present owner, you or your lawyer must ask to see proof that an *Escritura* has been made in the name of the inheritor and that any death duties have been paid.

This is important because if the property is still in the name of the deceased, you cannot obtain an *Escritura* in your name. You could also inherit problems over death duties if they are unpaid. My advice in these cases is to consult a Spanish lawyer.

As regards contracts for the purchase of a country or inherited property, you should follow the procedures explained in Chapter 1 for buying a resale property.

Chapter 4: Escritura title deed costs

COSTS for an *Escritura* title deed vary with the value of the property and the purchase price declared on the document. They also depend on where you are buying, as transfer taxes are set by provincial governments (Málaga, Murcia, Valencia, Madrid, Tenerife, Alicante etc).

It was once the custom in Spain to under-declare the purchase price, commonly by about 30%, in which case a property sold in reality for 200,000 Euros would appear to have changed hands for only 140,000 Euros.

Aware of this, and even in a downturn, the tax authorities have been valuing properties at much higher 'official' levels for the purposes of calculating charges. So although a seller may ask you to under-declare the price, my advice is to declare the full amount. The reason for being honest being the best policy is easy to follow.

The Land Registry will compare the value declared on your *Escritura* against their tables of values for properties of this type in your area. If they decide that your declared value is lower than their valuation, they can demand a supplementary charge on the difference as well as administration charges, postage and fines.

So let us say that your declare a sales price of 140,000 Euros on a house that the Land Registry deems to be worth 200,000 Euros, then you can be charged an additional 4,800 Euros, i.e. 8% of the 60,000 Euros difference, as well as administration charges and postage. It will be more if taxes add up to more than 8% in a locality.

Due to current oversupply and weak demand in the Spanish market, prices have dropped dramatically since 2008, so it is possible that even if you declare the true amount paid, the tax authorities may still place a higher value on the property you have purchased.

In one recent example: a property in Málaga was declared at a value of

45,076 Euros but the *Junta de Andalucía* inspected it and valued it at 81,137 Euros.

The tax on the difference and a hefty fine imposed on top added up to 7,212 Euros, approximately 6,556 British pounds. Had the correct amount been declared in the first place, the total cost for the difference would have been 2,524, approximately 2,295 British pounds.

You need to be aware too that if the declared value is 50% less than the official valuation, you can be forced to sell the property to the authorities for the declared value. It would be a heavy punishment and, as far as I know, this has never happened. But it pays to seek advice from your lawyer or the Notary's office to avoid your own story becoming a famous case study!

As an example of how the Land Registry values property, the tax authorities where I live set a minimum declared value in 2004 of 2.0 times the *Valor Catastral*, the rateable value of the property. This multiplier can go up or down each year. In 2005 it rose to 2.2, stayed the same in 2006, jumped to 2.7 in 2008, and is down again to 1.8 in 2012. There may also be regional variations. For example, they may well use different calculations in the provinces of Valencia and Málaga, so be advised by your lawyer.

As a rule of thumb, on a resale property the costs of the *Escritura* will be equivalent to around 9% of the total price of the property. So for our 200,000 Euros house you might expect the *Escritura* costs to be in the region of 18,000 Euros.

On a property being built for you, these costs may be greatly increased if you also have to pay the *Escritura* for the land purchase, the administrative segregation of your plot from the rest of the land, and the official declaration of a new building at the Notary's office.

Depending on the category of property being purchased, the breakdown of costs of an *Escritura of CompraVenta* is as follows.

1: For a resale property

- Transfer Tax on the declared value varies regionally: in 2012, they range from 6% to 10% depending on province, type of property and price band (Appendix A, page 128).
- Notary's fees for preparing the *Escritura* and legalising the document are charged on a sliding scale according to the declared value of the property and the number of pages in the *Escritura*.
- A deposit for the Land Registry office of approximately 0.5% of the declared value.
- *Plus Valia.* This is a tax levied by the *Ayuntamiento*, the Town Hall, which assesses you on the increase in the value of the land since the previous owner bought the property and subsequently sold it to you. So usually, the longer the people you are buying from have owned the property, the greater this tax will be. The law states that the person selling the property should pay the *Plus Valia* tax. But to ensure that it really is paid, I would suggest that the amount owing for the *Plus Valia* should be retained by your lawyer from the final payment to the vendor. One reason for this is that if the property is foreign owned and the sellers are returning to their country after the signing, what guarantee do you have that the *Plus Valia* will be paid. Under recent legislation, the local Town Hall can embargo the property purchased if the *Plus Valia* tax is unpaid, even if it was previously agreed that the vendor would pay this.

2: For a new property

When buying a property off-plan from a Developer/Builder, or a property under construction, or a new property which is finished but has never been inhabited, the *Escritura* costs are:

- IVA (value added tax) at 7% of the declared value of the property is paid to the Developer/Builder prior to signing the *Escritura*. The exception is in the Canary Islands, where the IVA is only 4.5%. Note that due to the sheer volume of unsold new properties in Spain, the national government reduced the 8% tax rate (7% I.V.A. & 1%

transfer tax) on new build properties down to 4% until the end of 2012.

- Stamp duty of 1 % on the declared value of the property.
- A deposit for the Land Registry of approximately 0.5% of the declared value of the property.
- *Plus Valia tax* as detailed above.

The rule of thumb for this when purchasing a new property is that total *Escritura* costs are an additional 1% more than when buying a resale property. So they could be around 20,000 Euros (10%) for our 200,000 Euros house. The figures above also apply to garages in the same place as the dwelling and purchased on the same date.

However, if the garage you are buying is in a different place, or is purchased on a different day, you pay 18% IVA and not 7%. Otherwise the figures are as detailed above. The 18% IVA rate also applies to buying **commercial premises**.

If you have not previously agreed that the Developer/Builder is responsible for the costs of the *Segregacion,* Segregation, the *Declaracion de Obra Nueva,* Declaration of a New Building, the *Division Horizontal,* Horizontal Division for an apartment, and the *Plus Valia* tax, you will pay much more. It is important that this is made clear in the Contract of Purchase & Sale.

3: Buying land and building your own property

Escritura costs here are greater because you are technically making two *Escrituras* - one for the land and, later, one for the new building. However, total costs are lower than buying a resale or new property purchased from a builder/developer. This is because you pay 8% transfer tax on the land value, but only 1 % tax for the building which is much higher value than the land.

The breakdown is:

- Transfer Tax of 8% of the declared value of the land.
- Notary's fees for preparing the *Escritura* and legalising it depend on the declared value of the land and the pages in the *Escritura*.
- A deposit for the Land Registry of approximately 0.5% of the declared value of the land.
- *Plus Valia* tax as previously detailed in this chapter.
- Once building is complete, go to the Notary to make a *Declaracion de Obra Nueva*, Declaration of a New Building. The costs for this *Escritura* are:
- Stamp Duty of 1% on the declared value of the new building.
- Notary's fees for preparing and legalising the document depend on the declared value of the building.
- A deposit for the Land Registry: around 0.5% of declared value.

There is no *Plus Valia* tax paid on declaration of a new building. You normally have 30 days after signing the *Escritura* to pay all costs. If you do not meet this deadline, there is normally a fine of 10% on the amount outstanding up to three months after the date of signing. Once three months have elapsed, the fine increases to 50%, so beware!

To save hassle, it is a good idea to deposit funds for the costs of the *Escritura* with your lawyer to pay on your behalf, and you should obviously be provided with an account and receipts of payment.

Remember that if you do not speak Spanish, are a foreigner in the country, do not know how the system works, you need to have employed a lawyer or registered *Gestor*.

Chapter 5: Community of Owners

IN THE United Kingdom and some other countries, local authorities are responsible for maintaining roads, green areas, and street lighting on a housing estate or around an apartment block.

In Spain though, the apartment block or *Urbanizacion,* housing estate, is completely private and the owners themselves are responsible for its upkeep. The law requires that a community of owners is formed and that each owner should pay proportionately towards the costs involved according to a formula that means some pay more than others.

The *Comunidad de Propietarios,* Community of Owners, is composed of all the owners of villas, apartments and business premises in the development complex.

They are responsible for paying for the maintenance of zones and items of common ownership, such as lighting in hallways in apartment blocks, communal gardens, swimming pools, and so on.

Taxes payable by the community as a whole are divided up among the owners and the *Comunidad* is also responsible for the promotion of harmony among its members.

An *Administrador de Fincas,* Administrator of Properties, is appointed by the community to deal with shared payments. This Administrator prepares annual accounts for community annual general meetings.

The amount each owner pays in community fees is set according to a 'quota of participation' in the community and the services that are included.

The quota of participation is determined by the size of your property. So for example, someone with a three bedroom property will have a higher quota and therefore a higher community fee than a neighbour with a one bedroom property.

Your quota is stated in the *Escritura* title deed, so you can easily check if the amount of participation is correct when assessing your community fees.

Some community fees include painting the exterior of the apartment block or all the villas/houses on a complex every two or three years. The community fees would be higher than on a complex where this is not included. If painting exteriors is included, the cost is normally spread over the two or three year period and extra payments are made during this time.

At the AGM, Annual General Meeting, which owners should be informed of well in advance, a President, Treasurer and Secretary will be elected by the owners from among themselves. You can also change or reappoint the Administrator at this meeting.

Complaints and suggestions have to be presented in writing to the Administrator of the community a reasonable length of time before the AGM for these issues to be voted on at the meeting.

It is very important for all owners to make an effort to attend the AGM, because all decisions taken at these meetings have legal force and will affect everyone in the community. If you are unable to attend, you should give somebody your proxy to vote on your behalf.

It is very important that all owners keep their community payments up to date. Failure to pay can result in your property being embargoed by the community of owners who may subsequently auction it at a knock-down price to recover outstanding debts.

Payment dates for community fees vary. You may find the community requests payments half-yearly or annually in advance.

If you are not resident in Spain, the most sensible course is to set up a standing order from your Spanish bank to pay on your behalf. Find out when payments are to be made so that you have enough in your account to cover them when they are due.

You should also ascertain what the annual community fees are before you sign the contracts, so you have an idea of what your annual outgoings are going to be. As I explained earlier, some community fees can be a considerable sum each year.

Get a copy of the statutes of the community so you know the rules and regulations that are binding on all owners before you become one. Your estate agent or lawyer should be able to help you do this.

Why bother? Well say you plan to live permanently in Spain and have a dog, but the community rules do not allow pets: it would be quite a problem if you had bought not knowing this.

It is also very important to establish if you need authorisation from the community to carry out any building work in the property, quite apart from needing a building licence from the Town Hall.

I have had cases where people have obtained a building permit from the Town Hall and started work only to be stopped by the community, which insisted on its own rules being followed.

Chapter 6: Power of Attorney

A POWER of Attorney (PoA) will be required if you or a joint purchaser cannot travel to Spain to sign the *Escritura* title deed.

Due to the relatively low cost of making a PoA in Spain, it really makes sense to sign one while you are in the country: when you are signing the contracts for example. That way, a PoA is already in place if you are unable to attend the Notary's personally for the signing of the *Escritura*.

If you do not have time to sign the PoA while in Spain, you will need a solicitor or a public Notary to prepare the PoA in Spanish and also in English if this is your language.

For this to be accepted in Spain, it must be in Spanish. Make sure that when the PoA is being drawn up it includes authorisation to obtain NIE foreigner identification numbers for you if you have not already obtained them.

If you are making the PoA in your country of residence, then once it has been signed, the public Notary must obtain an Apostille Certificate from the Foreign & Commonwealth Office (in the case of the United Kingdom). An Apostille is an official certificate that allows documents to be recognised in all European Union member states without further legal certification.

The Apostille should be attached to the PoA to authenticate it in Spain. However, if you make the PoA at a Spanish Consulate in your country of residence, there is no need for an Apostille. When you sign a PoA at a Spanish Consulate, it is regarded as being the same as if you had signed the document in Spain.

Your Notary will no doubt send the PoA to the Foreign & Commonwealth Office for the Apostille to be attached for you, but do allow some time for this process to be completed.

If you have to make the PoA in the UK and have no idea where to go, try contacting the nearest Spanish Consulate to ask them for the name, address and telephone number of a Spanish speaking public Notary in your area. If you are obtaining the PoA in the UK you could contact one of the UK law firms listed at the back of this book. The cost of preparing a PoA in the UK or elsewhere will be considerably more than in Spain - in the region of £200 to £400 plus the Notary's fees and the cost of the Apostille - and much more complicated.

To make a PoA in Spain, go along to the local Notary's office, provide personal and passport details, and tell them what you want the PoA for and to whom you are giving power of attorney.

The cost of a Special PoA is 70 to 80 Euros depending on the number of pages. A Special PoA will authorise a named person only to buy or sell a specified property for you, nothing more.

If you make a General PoA, costing around 90 to 120 Euros depending on the number of pages, this authorises a designated person to do almost anything on your behalf: buy or sell property, apply for loans, obtain a mortgage, whatever. In my opinion, and in the majority of cases, it is sufficient to make a Special PoA.

Remember that if you decide to make the PoA at a Spanish Consulate in your own country then there is no need for an Apostille. When you sign the PoA in the Spanish Consulate it is regarded as the same as if you had signed the document in Spain.

Chapter 7: Spanish Wills and Inheritance Tax

IT IS always sensible to make a last Will & Testament. If you are buying a property in Spain, I would go as far as to argue that it is essential for your long-term peace of mind and that of your family.

Under Spanish law, a third of the property automatically passes to the children on the death of either the husband or wife. However, your own country's laws normally override Spanish law and you may leave your estate according to your national laws.

To repeat this for clarity: if you do not make a last Will & Testament in Spain, but you have made one in your own country, the Will made in your country of residence would suffice in Spain. But there is potentially a big problem all the same.

This is because it would almost certainly create a Probate situation, as your country's inheritance laws would have to be proved and all documents would have to be officially translated. So to save complications, it makes sense to make a Will in Spain when you are buying property there.

I had a case once where I sold a property owned by a husband, wife and their two sons. A contract of purchase and sale had been signed and a deposit paid, but the mother died before the *Escritura* title deed was signed and did not have a Will & Testament in Spain.

I put them in touch with a very good lawyer in London who got all the documentation together reasonably rapidly to deal with the probate situation which had been created, and within six months the family were able to sign the acceptance of the inheritance document.

There was considerable delay beyond the original completion date for the sale, but the very understanding purchasers were prepared to wait for the situation to be resolved so that we could make the *Escritura* in their names. We were fortunate that they were patient, but it demonstrates why I stress the importance of making a Will & Testament in Spain.

The estate agent or lawyer that you are dealing with will be able to arrange Will(s) to be signed at the same time as you are signing the

Escritura, or it could be done when signing the contracts of Sale & Purchase, assuming there is enough time to prepare your Wills.

Under recent Spanish legislation, Wills are now prepared in two columns: one column in Spanish and the second in your own language.

The translation should in theory be done by an official translator; but generally speaking, the Notary will accept a translation made by someone known to have a good command of both languages.

If you are **buying in joint names**, you both need to make Wills, and each will cost approximately 200 Euros to cover the translation and the Notary's fees for preparing the Wills, presiding over the signing, and legalising them.

After the signing, you are given a *copia simple,* a simple copy of the original but without signatures. The original signed copy remains in the Notary's office.

The Notary sends a document to a central registry with details of the numbers of the Wills, the signing dates, your names, and at what time they were signed. No details of the contents are divulged.

If single or joint owners should die in a country other than Spain, the surviving partner or children will need to have an Apostille attached to the Death Certificate.

In the United Kingdom, an Apostille is obtained from the Foreign & Commonwealth Office. The certificate and Apostille are then sent or handed to the lawyer or *Gestoria Administrativa* dealing with the inheritance in Spain, along with a copy of the deceased person's Will & Testament. On receipt of the death certificate with the Apostille attached an official translation of the death certificate can be made. This will almost certainly be cheaper than having it translated in your own country.

You can avoid this time and expense if you are able to get a multilingual International Death Certificate (IDC) in you own official translation in Spain.

Your *Gestor* or lawyer who will present the last Will & Testament to the Notary's, asking them to request a certificate of *Ultimas Voluntades* (the last registered Will & Testament) from the central register.

When the Notary's office receives the certificate of *Ultimas Voluntades* your *Gestor* or lawyer can then present the death certificate, duly translated, and a copy of the *Escritura* title deed of the deceased person's property. This allows the Notary's office to prepare the new *Escritura* in the name of the inheritors.

You have a maximum period of six months to present the necessary documents to the tax authorities and you will of course have to pay death duties on the inheritance. The amount to pay and the discounts allowed are complex, as are the inheritance taxes that are applied.

As a rough idea, if the person or persons inheriting are husband/wife or children of the deceased, they may inherit 15,957 Euros per person free of tax. You will also be able to deduct funeral costs.

The amount that can be inherited free of tax by a person who is permanently disabled is much greater than the figure quoted, however you would need to check with your *Gestor* regarding this.

The percentage of tax payable on the taxable balance is on a complicated scale ranging from 7.65% to 34.00%. The best thing to do is to consult with either your lawyer, your *Gestor,* or your fiscal adviser.

In the region of *Andalucía,* which covers virtually the whole of Southern Spain, there have been major changes in inheritance tax for residents. If direct family members are inheriting the property, if they hold valid *Residencias,* and if they receive no more than 175,000 Euros per person, there may be no inheritance tax.

On top of inheritance taxes, you have the lawyer's or *Gestor's* fees for presenting and paying these taxes, plus costs for making a new *Escritura* for the property. **Death does not come cheap in Spain.**

One way of avoiding death duties is to put the property in the name/s of your child/children. This tactic is called **Usu Fructo** in Spanish law and your child/children would have to sign the contracts of *CompraVenta* Purchase & Sale Contract.
The Notary must also be advised of this when preparing the *Escritura* title deeds. If you do buy in your child/children's names, with you having *Usu Fructo,* rights of use, your child/children must either sign the *Escritura* with you or give you or your lawyer a Power of Attorney to sign on their behalf.

By retaining lifelong rights of use, you cannot be refused access to the property and the child/children cannot sell it without your signature/s on the *Escritura.* You are entitled to rent the property and receive the income.

Once you have made a Will & Testament in Spain, there is no need to make another if you sell a property and buy another. This is because the Will states that it covers anything you own in Spain at the time of death: property, stocks and shares, cash at the bank, and so on.

The Will & Testament that you make in Spain is purely for Spanish territory - the mainland, the Balearic & the Canary Islands - and does not affect Wills made in the UK or other countries.

If you make a Will in Spain then make a new one or change your existing Will in your country of residence or any other country, you must add a proviso that the new Will does not affect any Wills made outside of that country, otherwise it would cancel your Spanish Will.

Usually, a Will made in Spain leaves the estate to a husband/wife and, on the death of both, to any children and, on the death of the children, to grandchildren. So the only time you need a new Will is if you wish to alter the beneficiaries or what they will inherit.

Chapter 8: Retiring, Residencia & Working

IF YOU are planning to live permanently in Spain, you should obtain *Residencia* (residency) and also get a *Certificado de Empadronamiento* by having your name put on the electoral register, *padrón,* at your Town Hall. You need to do this to register for free care under the Spanish Health Service.

If your are younger than the Spanish retirement age, see page 13 for *Residencia* and *Empadronamiento*.

If you are of retirement age, you qualify for an S1, previously known as an E121, with which you can register with the Spanish health authorities and receive reciprocal free health care under the Spanish Social Security system. If you are a pensioner you will also receive other benefits, such as reduced fares on public transport.

If you are of **retirement age and British**, contact the Pensions Service in Newcastle (tel: +44 (0)191 218 7777) to see if you qualify for an S1. Previously it would have been sufficient to have been paying your National Insurance (NI) contributions for a specified period. Now, you must be of retirement age.

Give them your UK NI number and tell them you are taking up permanent residence in Spain. If you qualify for an S1, then when you have purchased property in Spain you contact the Pensions Service again, giving them your address to send the S1 to you.

If you are of **another nationality but part of the EU**, contact the pension authorities in your own country about the S1 document.

On receipt of the S1, and having previously received your *Residencia* and *Empadronamiento,* armed also with your passport and copies of all these documents, go to the nearest offices of *Seguridad Social,* Social Security, which is normally attached to one of the *ambulatorios* (local clinics or cottage hospitals), and register yourself with the Spanish

Health Service.

They will issue a paper card, a *tarjeta de afiliacion*. Take this to your nearest *ambulatorio* to register with a doctor. You will be issued with a plastic card at a later date. This card, the *tarjeta sanitaria individualizada nacional,* can be used to access health care under the Spanish state run health service.

If the authorities are unable to provide you with the relevant cards at the time you apply, you will receive interim papers to confirm that your application is being processed.

Health care cover commences from the day you register your S1. In some circumstances, registration may take several months. So you should:

• Present the S1 as soon as possible: do not wait until you need treatment, as you may be charged and these costs may not be refunded.

• Ask the Spanish authorities to apply to your home country's health authorities – in Newcastle if you are British – for S1 cover if you have dependent family members living with you.

If you have a UK passport, plan to stay in Spain for a reasonable length of time, but not more than 183 days, and do not intend taking up *Residencia*, you can obtain an EHIC (European Health Insurance Card), previously known as an E111.

You can do this either online at www.nhs.uk/healthcareabroad or by ringing the Pensions Service on +44 (0)191 218 7777 (or 0845 6050707 within the UK) to apply for the EHIC, which is similar in size to a credit card and is valid for five years. You will need one for each family member. This gives temporary medical cover while you are in Spain or any other EU country.

If you are **from another EU member state**, contact the authorities in your home country to obtain the EHIC card.

If you are **not of legal retirement age** and therefore do not qualify for an S1 from the UK, or you are not employed or self-employed, you will of course need **private health insurance** (PHI). Or it may be that you are working or self-employed and would like the added cover of PHI anyhow. Various schemes are available in Spain and your policy should cover all aspects of health care, to include doctors, hospitalisation, and so on.

For some idea of PHI costs, I asked my local office of insurance company Mapfre, one of the largest in Spain. This is what I gleaned.

Costs vary with age and if applying individually or as a couple, or if taking cover for the whole family. It is impossible to cover all age groups and families, but here are some typical quotes, rounded up to the nearest Euro, for standard PHI policies from late 2011.

- Man, age 34: 59 Euros per month (p/m)
- Woman, age 26: 69 Euros p/m
- Joint PHI for husband, age 32, and wife, age 28: 133 Euros p/m
- Family cover for man, age 32, wife, age 30, and kids, ages three and five: 248 Euros p/m
- Family cover for man, 42, wife 40, and their children, ages 10 and 14: 246 Euros p/m
- Family cover for man, age 51, wife, age 53, son, age 22: 246 Euros p/m

If you have PHI cover in your own country, check to see if this covers you in Spain. Many PHI companies have Spanish subsidiaries, so you may well be able to transfer the policy to Spain. If so, check if you need any other documentation to ensure that you are covered in Spain and if there are costs.

Working as an Employee - *Cuenta Ajena*

If you are an EU citizen and have the right to live and work in Spain, then if you are working, whether employed or self employed, you are not obliged to apply for *Residencia*, though I have explained why I think you should do so anyhow.

Looking for work in Spain? Then go to a local office of the *Instituto Nacional de Empleo* (INEM) to register as *demandante de empleo*, seeking employment. They advise of any available work. If you find employment without INEM, you must let them know so they can remove you from their database.

Your employer must give you a copy of the contract that you have both signed, detailing all terms and conditions of employment. The company or person employing you, or their *Gestoria Administrativa*, should help you register with the Social Security. Once you have your Social Security card, you should also go along to the nearest *ambulatorio* to register with a doctor.

You must get a *Numero de Identificacion Extranjero* (NIE), the Foreigner Identification Number which is also your tax number in Spain. If you are going to apply for *Residencia*, you do not need to apply for the NIE separately as this will be issued along with your *Residencia*, so it makes sense to apply for the *Residencia* immediately (page 13).

Where you obtain the *Residencia* and NIE from varies from one town to another. It is normally the *Departamento de Extranjeros*, Foreigners' Department, at a National Police Station.

Your employer's *Gestoria Administrativa* should also be prepared to take you to apply for the *Residencia* and your NIE, which of course can be applied for at the same time. They will probably make a small charge for doing so, but it can save you a lot of frustration.

You will need to fill in an application form and present it duly filled in, plus a photocopy, along with form known as a Modelo 790 which you should take to the bank and pay in 10.20 Euros per application prior to presenting the form to pay for your *Residencia* and NIE.
This fee could change or vary from one part of Spain to another, so

please take it simply as a guide. You will also need your passport, a photocopy of the passport page that has your photograph on it, and a *Certificado de Empadronamiento,* a certificate from the local Town Hall showing you are registered on the electoral register. Your *Gestoria Administrativa* can supply you with the application and tax forms.

Self Employed (*Cuenta Propia*)

If you plan to start a business then you need to register with the tax authorities and Social Security and get an NIE number. You will need the help of a *Gestoria Administrativa/Graduado Social* to deal with registering you and then to deal with your own social security payments and tax returns. Look for the 'GA' sign outside the Gestoria's door. You will also need their help with contracts, payroll and social security for any staff that you plan to employ.

Chapter 9: Business Premises

A HUGE number of people visit Spain on holiday and imagine it would be great to live there. They think to themselves: 'We could buy a little bar, spend time on the beach, take it easy, no stress like we have back home.' The reality of running any business in Spain is far removed from this dream of the good life, particularly now.

Take the pub trade. In the summer, a bar needs to be open seven days a week and all hours of the day and night to produce enough income to see the owners through the usually much slower winter months. Competition is fierce too: there are just so many bars, cafeterias and restaurants fighting for custom.

Take unscheduled days off to go to the beach instead of opening regularly, particularly in the summer months, and you will soon wonder where all your business went. So think very carefully before buying this type of business.

You can certainly expect little leeway from landlords if you run into trouble. Commercial rents just seem to go up and up. They are rarely cut, as many Spanish landlords would rather see a property lie empty than accept a rent that means they return to a low base for future rent negotiations.

Also, many town and village properties are owned by individuals or families rather than commercial landlords with large portfolios. So the family's income that is used to house, feed, educate, heal and entertain itself, and pay its debts, is likely to come in large or significant part from the rent that you are paying. If they have high costs, they need to cover them from the rent on their commercial property, particularly when little paid work is now available for many people in Spain, especially away from the cities.

If you really do plan to start a business in Spain, do not rush into it. Spend some time looking around to see what you think is lacking in the area where you plan to live, then set up a business that you think has a fair chance of being successful.

Once you have found premises to rent or buy – and it may be an existing business - you will certainly need the help of a recommended lawyer to deal with the contracts and a *Gestoria Administrativa*, fiscal advisers to handle the paperwork, opening licences, registering with the tax authorities, social security, and so on.

If the premises are on offer through an increasingly rare leasehold known as a *traspaso*, an indefinite lease, ask your lawyer/*Gestoria Administrativa* to do their best to ensure that this right is not cancelled when signing contracts.

The other type of contract, a *cesion*, is purely a rental agreement and is normally for a period of one year but renewable for up to five years. Rent is typically reviewed each year and should be increased only by the percentage rise in the official cost of living index published each January by the government.

Both types of contract should give the renter the right to resell the business in the premises to a third party. One of the questions that serious business people ask before they start up is how they will get out if they want or have to.

With either a *traspaso* or *cesion*, you may find that the landlord will want a clause stating that he will receive anything between 10% and 30% of the price that you sell the business in those premises for.

Your lawyer should negotiate this percentage with the landlord on your behalf when preparing the contracts. Remember that the landlord may well want to renegotiate the rent with the new owners of the business, so this may affect what you might reasonably say to prospective buyers when marketing the business for sale.

Before committing yourself to buy either a *Traspaso* or a *Cesion*, you and your lawyer need to meet with the owner of the premises to discuss rent and the terms and conditions of the new contract.

At the end of the term of a *Cesion* you have a right of renewal but must renegotiate the rent. Your lawyer should be present at negotiations with the owner when the contract is being renewed.

Before you commit to signing contracts, your lawyer or *Gestoria Administrativa* should also check out what type of business opening licence has been issued by the *Ayuntamiento,* Town Hall.

I have come across a case, for example, where the premises only had an opening licence for a supermarket, yet the landlord/owners had converted them into a bar and sold the freehold or lease at an attractively low price.

The person who bought it discovered too late that the Town Hall would only authorise use as a supermarket. They had no choice but to convert it back to a supermarket, which cost a lot of money and time. So tread very carefully and, I repeat, use the services of a recommended lawyer.

If you are renting/leasing premises, you must retain 19% of the rental paid to the owner (more from September 2012). This retention, which you pay instead to the Tax Authorities, may well have been introduced originally because many landlords/owners were not declaring rental income.

If the premises already have an opening licence, it may well be that you can simply transfer this to your name at the *Ayuntamiento,* Town Hall. Even this can take time though and different local authorities take different views on whether you can run the business in the interim.

If the premises you are leasing/renting/buying are new, or you are making alterations to them, you will need detailed plans drawn up by an *Ingeniero Tecnico Industrial,* Industrial Technical Engineer, and these must be stamped and approved by the *Colegio Oficial de Ingenieros Industriales,* The Official College of Industrial Engineers.

Once you have these plans you must present them to the *Ayuntamiento* and pay for the licence. Your lawyer or *Gestoria Administrativa* will deal with the transfer of the opening licence or organise the Industrial Technical Engineer for you.

You must also obtain an NIE number and a *Licencia Fiscal,* Fiscal

Licence, registering you with the Tax Authorities, and must also register with the *Seguridad Social,* Social Security, and make Social Security payments. You will need a *Gestoria Administrativa* and Fiscal Adviser to deal with these issues, and your lawyer should be able to recommend who to use.

If you have a rental contract for the premises, your lawyer or *Gestor* should also ensure that it is registered in the *Camara de la Propiedad,* Registry of Rented Property, and stamped as registered.

If your business involves handling food – a café, restaurant or gastro-pub maybe - you must sit an examination on all the dos and don'ts of dealing with food. This is known as a food handling licence. It is certainly not difficult. Most of the exam is based on common sense. But you should prepare for it and will receive a certificate for your efforts.

If buying the freehold on a business property, the documentation and the clauses in the contracts should be pretty much the same as for buying a resale property, as stated in Chapter 1.

Again, you would be well advised to use the services of a recommended lawyer to deal with the contracts and to ensure that the premises have the correct licences for the business that you are intending to set up.

Chapter 10: Spanish Driving Licences

IF YOU are planning to drive while you are temporarily in Spain, you should take your current driving licence with you.

If you are going to live in Spain permanently and will apply for *Residencia,* then EU regulations mean that you no longer need to exchange your own driving licence for a Spanish one.

However, my advice is nevertheless to obtain a Spanish driving licence, because the Spanish Police could still give you some hassle if they stop you for some reason. The Spanish driving licence bears your photograph while the older style UK licences still used by many British citizens have nothing to show what they look like.

As far as the authorities are concerned, if you have residential status in Spain then you have the same standing as a Spanish citizen, so you should have a Spanish driving licence. It is really in your own interest.

To obtain your Spanish driving licence you have to hand in your current licence, which is not returned to you. Your current driving licence is retained by the authorities because they now regard you no differently than if you were a Spanish driver.

When applying for your Spanish driving licence you will need your current driving licence, duly signed, a photocopy of your *Residencia,* a copy of your *Escritura* title deed or property rental contract and four passport size photographs, which must be on a white background.

If your address for some reason is now different to your *Residencia* card, you will need a *Certificado de Empadronamiento* from your local Town hall to show that you are permanently residing at this latest address.

When you apply for your Spanish licence, you could do so yourself, but my advice is to contact a *Gestoria Administrativa* and ask them to deal with it for you, even if you are pretty fluent in Spanish. Dealing with the traffic authorities can be a very lengthy and complicated process and: even the Spanish are wary about dealing with *Trafico.*

Renewing a driving licence

From **18 to 65 years of age**, the licence is renewed every 10 years
From **65 years of age**, it is renewed every 5 years

Before your licence expires, *Trafico* will send a renewal form to your Spanish address advising you that you can renew it by post. To do this you will need the following documents:

• A medical certificate issued by an approved medical centre and on which a passport size photograph must be attached.

• A photocopy of your *Residencia* or your passport or NIE certificate.

• Your expired driving licence.

• Two passport size photographs taken against a white background

• A stamped addressed envelope bearing your address.

• The bottom part of the renewal form sent by *Trafico*.

• A giro made payable to *Trafico* for the amount stated on the renewal form (approximately 16 Euros). There is no charge for people aged 70 or more.

When you go for the straightforward medical examination, they will give you an eye test. If you need glasses to pass this test, you must also be wearing the glasses on the passport size photographs that you present. If you need glasses for driving, you are legally bound to carry a spare set in the car at all times and may be fined if you don't.

Send all the documents by registered post to the *Trafico* office for your area. It may take a few weeks for your new licence to arrive, so you must carry the remaining part of the renewal form sent by *Trafico* along with the receipt for the giro transfer payment.

It is also advisable to take a photocopy of your old licence to carry with you until you receive the new one, just in case the renewal gets lost in the post. If you were to be stopped by the police, you could show them the renewal form and a copy of your old licence.

You could go yourself to the *Trafico* offices to renew your licence, but my advice is to deal with it by post or get a *Gestoria Administrativa* to do it for you.

General Obligations for Drivers

Private cars may not travel faster than 50 kilometres per hour (kph) in urban areas and 120 kph on motorways and dual-carriageways.

It is obligatory to have: a driving licence; valid comprehensive or third party insurance; proof of payment of the insurance, and original identification documents for the vehicle, namely the technical inspection card and traffic permit.

Photocopies of these documents are admissible only if certified by either a Notary at a cost of approximately 6 Euros per page; or the Municipal Police, *Trafico* itself, or some Banks. These documents must be carried at all times when you are driving.

It is obligatory to wear a seat belt in both the front and rear of a car and a crash helmet when on a motorbike, scooter or moped.

You must have two red triangles in the boot of the car. In the event of a breakdown on a single carriageway, one is to be placed in front of the vehicle and the other behind at a distance of about 10 metres from where it must be visible from 100 metres. If the breakdown is on a dual carriageway, such as a motorway, you need only place the triangle that goes behind the vehicle.

You are also obliged to have two authorised, reflective vests in the car and these must be put on before leaving the vehicle if you break down.

If you commit a breach of traffic regulations outside the urban area and you get a fine, such as for speeding, you will have a 20% discount if you pay the fine within 20 days. Serious fines do not qualify. Payments of fines are made at the *Trafico* offices, usually in the main city of the province, or at Banco Santander.

Chapter 11: Mortgages

MORTGAGES are available in Spain. Most Spanish home owners have variable rate loans where the interest rate is changed annually. There is a wide range, but to give you and an idea of what was on offer recently, I went to my local branch of **Banco Sabadell**.

I choose it as an example because it specialises in non-resident mortgages, mainly through its **Banco Sabadell** branches, though it also offers home loans to residents, and all **SabadellSolbank** branches throughout Spain have multilingual staff. Of course, their offer also covers day-to-day banking, finance for non-resident customers, and all the financial needs of Spanish residents.

Banco Sabadell lends up to 70% of either the bank's valuation of the property or the purchase price, whichever is lower, with a maximum term of 40 years and subject to financial status. You need to be older than 18, have a regular stable income, and be able to show that you can afford the mortgage.

Basic mortgage types include **Variable Rate**, **Fixed Rate**, and **Mixed Rate**

1. Variable Rate Mortgages

This kind of loan allows you to take advantage of falling rates, though obviously, it also incorporates rises. The main advantage is that it is adjusted every 12 months to match market rates. The maximum term of the loan is 40 years and the oldest you can be at the end of the mortgage period is 75 years old.

The interest rate applied is variable. It may be based on a financial index known as the *Indice de Prestamos Hipotecarios-conjunto de Entidades (IPRHce),* an average rate for all mortgages from Spanish financial institutions which is published by Spain's central bank, Banco de España. Or it may depend on EURIBOR, the European Interbank Offered Rate, which is published by the European Central Bank and is a rate at which banks lend to each other short-term. Monthly repayments on this mortgage are a fixed amount, adjusted once a year.

Prepayment fee: (% of prepaid amount): 0.50% during the first 5 years of the mortgage, 0.25% the remaining years.

Bonus Mortgage: If you would like interest rate discounts you may open a Prestige Care Account and entrust the bank with your home and life insurance; but **please note** that the insurance policy is available only to residents of the European Economic Area and Russia.

2. Fixed Rate Mortgages

If you do not wish to be concerned about interest rate changes, a Fixed Rate Mortgage assures constant monthly payments for the life of the loan.

The maximum term of the loan is 30 years and the oldest you can be at the end of the mortgage period is 75 years old. Monthly repayments are fixed during the entire life of the mortgage. If you wish to benefit from lower repayments during the initial years, their **Different Mortgage** may fit your needs

Prepayment Fee (0% of prepaid amount): 0.50% during the first 5 years of the mortgage, 0.25% the remaining years. When the early repayment causes a financial loss to the lender an interest rate risk fee of 4% will be charged.

3. Mixed Rate Mortgages

If you want to avoid possible interest rate rises during the first years of a mortgage but are prepared to accept adjustments longer-term, then a mixed rate mortgage may be the answer.

The maximum term of the loan is 40 years and the oldest you can be at the end of the mortgage period is 75 years old. Monthly payments are made at a fixed interest rate for the first four years. Thereafter the rate is adjusted once a year.

Prepayment fee (0% of prepaid amount): 0.50% during the first 5 years of the mortgage, 0,25% the remaining years. When the early repayment causes a financial loss to the lender an interest rate of 4% will be charged.

MORGAGE PAYMENT CALCULATOR							
Rate (%)	10 Years	15 Years	20 Years	25 Years	30 Years	35 Years	40 Years
3.00	9.66	6.91	5.55	4.74	4.22	3.85	3.58
3.25	9.77	7.03	5.67	4.87	4.35	3.99	3.73
3.50	9.89	7.15	5.80	5.01	4.49	4.13	3.87
3.75	10.01	7.27	5.93	5.14	4.63	4.28	4.03
4.00	10.12	7.40	6.06	5.28	4.77	4.43	4.18
4.25	10.24	7.52	6.19	5.42	4.92	4.58	4.34
4.50	10.36	7.65	6.33	5.56	5.07	4.73	4.50
4.75	10.48	7.78	6.46	5.70	5.22	4.89	4.66
5.00	10.61	7.91	6.60	5.85	5.37	5.05	4.82
5.25	10.73	8.04	6.74	5.99	5.52	5.21	4.99
5.50	10.85	8.17	6.88	6.14	5.68	5.37	5.16
5.75	10.98	8.30	7.02	6.29	5.84	5.54	5.33
6.00	11.10	8.44	7.16	6.44	6.00	5.70	5.50
6.25	11.23	8.57	7.31	6.60	6.16	5.87	5.68
6.50	11.35	8.71	7.46	6.75	6.32	6.04	5.85
6.75	11.48	8.85	7.60	6.91	6.49	6.21	6.03

Source: **Banco Sabadell**

How to use the table? Look at the first column and find the annual interest rate that you have been offered. Now move along that row until you find the monthly repayment for the term of the loan in years. This is the monthly repayment for each 1,000 Euros that you wish to borrow. For instance a 200,000 Euros mortgage loan at 6% for 10 years means a monthly repayment of approximately 2,220 Euros (11.10 x 200). We say approximately because we have rounded monthly repayments in the table to the nearest euro cent to make it easier to read. The actual repayment in this example would be 2,220.41 Euros (11.102050 x 200).

Get a quote: Lenders should provide a free, fully detailed quotation of the mortgage payments and your loan and purchase expenses. Ask for this at a branch in Spain or by calling a mortgage centre. In **Banco Sabadell's** case, the mortgage centre telephone is **+34 902 343 999** and the website **bancsabadell.com/en**

Documentation

They will need the following documentation and original documents must be shown before signing a mortgage or purchase contract:

- Identity card or passport.
- Your last two pay-slips if you are salaried. Or proof of payments of income tax through your bank account in the current year if you are self-employed.
- Your last income tax return (Form P60 in the UK or the equivalent tax statement elsewhere).
- Your latest full tax return if this is applicable.
- A banking reference.
- Property related documents: the private purchase contract for a new property or the *Escritura* title deed for a re-sale property.
- An Experian file or Credit report.
- Your application and queries should be handled quickly and efficiently. In **Banco Sabadell**'s case, they promise a response within 48 hours.

Self-build mortgage

Mortgages may be available to self-build a new home. For example, **Banco Sabadell** lends up to 70% of project costs, to draw down in stages. The minimum age at the start of the loan is 18 and the oldest you can be when the mortgage expires is 75.

The loan must be drawn down in full, and construction completed, within about 18 months of first draw-down. A surveyor acceptable to the bank is appointed to monitor and approve construction stages. Staged draw-downs are released on receipt of relevant certification from this surveyor. Completed property is re-valued by a bank appointed valuer.

Non-banking expenses

Costs incurred before you apply for a mortgage include the **valuation fee** and assorted **additional costs and legal fees**.

Valuation fee - *Tasacion*

The maximum amount of loan depends on the property value, so the bank needs a valuation done by a bank approved valuer.

Additional costs & legal fees

When you buy property with or without a mortgage loan, Spanish Law stipulates compulsory costs to ensure no problems when the final transaction is made. There is also the tax office to satisfy. These expenses and taxes have nothing to do with the bank and are usually equivalent to 11% of the purchase price (7% transfer tax or IVA for the purchase itself, 3% for any mortgage needed, Notary and Land Registry fees). Include these in your budget to avoid unpleasant surprises. They include:

- Your own legal fees
- The bank's legal fees
- Resale property transfer tax, payable on the purchase and the mortgage
- New build property IVA (equivalent to Value Added Tax in the UK)
- Land Registry fees payable on both the purchase and the mortgage.
- Notary's fees payable on both the purchase and the mortgage.
- Valuation fees.
- Arrangement fees.

Ensure that your lawyer provides a detailed breakdown of all costs prior to commencing the transaction.

Bank fees

Banco Sabadell charges an arrangement fee between 1% and 1.5% of the mortgage – subject to a minimum of 750 Euros - depending on the acquisition of other **Banco Sabadell** products and services. Valuation fees and a fixed rate reservation fee will also apply. The bank has further details.

Legal advice

You need a lawyer to bring together all the documentation at the appropriate time. The lawyer will advise on obtaining legal title to the property and is responsible for providing a detailed breakdown of purchase costs, which are separate to mortgage arrangement charges.

Insurance and protection

Fire insurance is compulsory for property used as collateral for a mortgage, but banks recommend considering at least two other policies. A Home Protection Plan is a comprehensive insurance for your property, while mortgage-related life insurance will cancel outstanding mortgage debt in the event of death or, optionally, permanent disability.

Securing a loan

A first charge over the property is required as security for the loan.

Signature

Once a bank has approved your application, you provide the following documents for them to take care of all the rest.

If you are buying a **new home from a developer** and applying for a mortgage on the property, the bank will need:

- A 'New Building Certificate' from the developer (*Licencia de Primera Ocupacion*)
- A photocopy of the private purchase contract or letter of offer.

If you are buying **an existing home** and applying for a mortgage, the bank will need a photocopy of the present owner's *Escritura* title deed.

If you are planning to **build your own home**, the bank will need:

- A photocopy of the deeds of the land or plot.

- A building project (*Un Proyecto de un Arquitecto*) stamped by the Architects' Association.

- The planning permission from the *Ayuntamiento*, Town Hall.

- The compulsory *Seguro Decenal* 10-year construction insurance.

All banks add **disclaimers** to their mortgage offers telling you where their responsibility stops and what you may and may not do. Check these carefully.

Banco Sabadell, for example, stipulates that in providing the services that I have tried to outline accurately in this book, the bank is not in any way acting as legal, tax and/or other professional advisers or giving legal, tax and/or other professional advice and they strongly recommend that you obtain independent, legal tax and/or other professional tax advice as appropriate.

Also, their services are not offered to any person in any jurisdiction where their advertisement, offer or sale is restricted by law or regulation or where they are not appropriately licensed.

Offers apply only to over 18s and are subject to status and conditions. Security is required on Spanish property. Written quotations are available. Calls to bank staff may be recorded. Internet e-mails are not necessarily secure as information might be intercepted, lost or destroyed. So please do not e-mail any account or other confidential information.

Your home may be repossessed if you do not keep up the repayments on your mortgage. You should check that a mortgage will meet your needs if you want to move or sell your home or you want your family to inherit it. If you are in any doubt, seek independent advice.

Changes in the exchange rate may increase the sterling or other currency equivalent of your debt. For mortgages with interest payments based upon variable rate terms there is a risk that the total sum payable under your mortgage increases significantly as rates rise.

Chapter 12: Spanish Property Taxes

THE ONLY certainties in life are death and taxes. I wish you long life, but **this chapter is required reading** and you really would be best using a *Gestoria Administrativa, Economista* (chartered accountant), or a lawyer, to handle tax issues.

I deal here almost exclusively with property related taxes. If you are tax resident in Spain, your income tax liabilities are beyond the scope of this book and my advice is to contact a recommended registered professional.

Non Residents Tax Law

Real Decreto Legislativo 5/2004 of the 5th. March and *Real Decreto 1776/2004 of the 30th. July*, are the latest laws containing all changes at the time this book was published, but as tax laws constantly change, you must check with your tax advisor.

Fiscal Identification Number (NIE)

Remember that all individuals and companies must have a Fiscal Identification Number for tax purposes. There is no discrimination between Spanish nationals or foreigners. In the case of foreign owners, the Fiscal Identification Number is known as *Numero Identificacion Extranjero* (NIE) and it is issued by the Foreigners' Department at your nearest National Police Station, or at any Spanish Consulate, a procedure explained in First Steps (page 12).

In the case of foreign owned companies, the Fiscal Identification Number is known as *Codigo de Identificacion Fiscal* (CIF) and is issued by the Spanish Tax Office.

A photocopy of the original NIE/CIF certificate must be presented at the Notary's office at the signing of the *Escritura* title deed: without the certificate, the transfer taxes cannot be paid when the *Escritura* is presented at the Land Registry office.

Fiscal Representatives

Non-resident owners are obliged by law to have a registered Fiscal Representative in the following cases;

* When a non-resident has a permanent base of activity in Spain.
* When the Spanish Tax Office requests you appoint a Fiscal Representative based on the amounts of the income obtained in Spain by the non-resident.
* For non-resident companies in all cases.

The Fiscal Representative should be a qualified professional such as a *Gestor Administrativo, Economista,* or a Lawyer.

If you need a Fiscal Representative, do check that they are registered with the relevant college. There are a number of individuals who act as Fiscal Representatives in Spain, but you should deal only with College Registered Professionals (There should be a plaque outside their office with their college registration number on).

Non-resident owners of properties

Here I discuss: properties that are not rented out; rented-out properties; and property rented out for only part of the year.

1: Properties not rented out

Every individual owning a property in Spain is liable for Non-Resident Income Tax, based on the *Valor Catastral* (Rateable Value) of the property. If there is no *Valor Catastral* then 50% of the *Escritura* value will be used instead. **The tax form that you will need is known as a 210-I**

Each owner on the *Escritura* title deed will pay their proportional share of the tax. The tax must be paid during the following year, for example you will be paying the tax in 2013 for the year 2012. The tax year in Spain runs from January 1 to December 31.

The town or village that your property is in will determine the percentage of tax that you have to pay.

If your Town Hall had **revised the Catastral Values before 1994**, the Tax Base is 2%.of the Catastral Value.

If your Town Hall had **revised the Catastral Value after 1994**, the tax base is 1.1% of the Catastral Value.

The tax rate is normally 24% of either the rateable value of 1.1% or 2% (however, for the tax years 2012 & 2013 the tax rate will be 24.75%).

As an example, if the *Valor Catastral* is 50,000 Euros, the income tax for the year 2011 would be 132 Euros (*Valor Catastral* 50.000 Euros x 1.1% x 24% = 132 Euros).

2: Rented-out properties

Taxes will be based on the **income** received from the rentals. **The tax form is: 210-R.** The tax rate is normally 24% but for the tax years 2012 & 2013 it will be 24.75% and payment is due quarterly.

So tax on rental income received during January, February and March must be paid between April 1 and 20. Tax on rental income received during April, May and June must be paid between the July 1 and 20.

Tax on rental income received during July, August and September must be paid between October 1 and 20. Tax on rental income received during October, November and December must be paid between the January 1 and 20 of the following year.

If the property is rented by a company, i.e. an estate agency or rental company the non resident taxes will be retained at source by that company.

3: Property rented out for only part of the year

The same non-resident income taxes apply.

You pay taxes on the proportional part of the *Valor Catastral* for the number of days that the property has not been rented, and use **Tax Form 210-I** for this.

For the number of days that the property has been rented out, you pay taxes based on the income obtained and use **Tax Form 210-R.**

Rented out by non-resident EU citizens

Since 2010, EU owners of Spanish property who are non-resident in Spain but are renting out their Spanish property have been able to offset expenses against income obtained, in the same way as for Spanish tax residents.

Deductable expenses are: the interest paid on a mortgage; *IBI* (property rates); community fees; insurance; electricity; water; maintenance; and, if it applies, refuse collection.

Applying for a refund of expenses for non-resident taxes withheld at source by a company can be done for up to four years.

Please note that since January 1, 2009, **there been no double taxation agreement with Denmark.** The Republic of **Cyprus is classed as a Fiscal Paradise,** an offshore tax haven.

Non-resident companies special taxes

All non-resident owned companies are liable to special taxes, which are 3% of the *Valor Catastral* per annum and must be paid in January of the following year. Use **Tax Form 213.**

Exemptions from this special tax are literally translated as follows:

* Foreign States or Public or International Institutions.

* Organisations with the right to apply an agreement with an information exchange clause and provided that the individuals who own the property are resident in Spain or in a country with an agreement of this type.

- Organisations that carry out financial operations other than simple building tenancy or rental.
- Companies listed in the officially recognised secondary securities markets.
- Non-profit organisations complying with legal requirements.

Non-resident property sellers

Any non-resident individual or company selling property will have 3% of the sale price retained by the purchaser as a deposit against assumed capital gains on the property.

The purchaser must pay this retention to the Tax Office within one month from the *Escritura* date. This sum becomes an encumbrance on the property purchased if it is not paid.

The non-resident vendor/s are obliged to pay any outstanding Capital Gains Tax (CGT) four months from the date of the sale.

For a non-resident vendor, the CGT rate is normally 19%, but during the years 2012 and 2013 IT will be 21% of the profit made on a sale.

Profit will be the difference between the purchase price plus the costs and taxes inherent in the acquisition and the value when sold, minus some allowable profits. **Use Tax Form 210-H.**

For a non-resident vendor who has not made any gain at the time of selling, there is the possibility of recovering the 3% retained. **Use Tax Form 210-H.**

If you are a vendor wishing **to reclaim any or all of the 3% of the sale price retained by the purchaser**, you must have paid your annual taxes.

If you have not made tax returns each year since you bought your property, the authorities in Spain will deduct them from the amount you are claiming and also levy fines for late payment, so you could well find that you will get nothing back. So you can see that **it is** very **important that you make tax returns each year** to avoid this happening.

Resident in Spain for tax purposes

If an individual (Spanish National or foreigner) stays in Spain for more that **183 days** in any calendar year, or if the **principal base** of their business and professional activities or economic interests are in Spain, then the tax authorities will assume, unless it is proved otherwise, that he or she is **tax resident in Spain**.

This assumption will be extended to a wife or husband, provided there is no legal separation or divorce, and any children who are under age and depend on you will also be deemed to live in Spain.

Temporary absences are taken into account in determining the period of your stay in Spain, unless you can prove that you habitually live in another country during 183 days of the calendar year.

Anyone else is considered **non-resident in Spain**.

All individuals resident in Spain will be liable for income tax on their worldwide income and assets under the applicable rules. This means declaring all properties owned, though a permanent home will be exempt from wealth taxes. Second and further properties will have to be declared, including any in another country. If they are not rented out, they will be taxed on their rateable value. They will be taxed on profits if they are rented out.

A company is considered resident in Spain for tax purposes if it is constituted under Spanish law, or has registered offices in Spain, or has a head office in Spain.

Foreign residents selling a property

When signing a sale, foreign residents selling property in Spain must prove they have tax resident status in Spain by presenting to the

Notary the certificate issued by the Spanish Tax Office.

A resident making a profit on sale of property is **liable for Capital Gains Tax (CGT)** But there is **an exemption from CGT for tax-resident sellers over 65 years of age on selling their home**. This recognises that they could be selling to supplement pensions or to move into a smaller property suited to their needs. **Resident sellers over 65 years of age selling their home** need to know this:

* Home is defined as the property where the vendor has been **living for at least the previous three years** up to the date of the sale. A *Certificado de Empadronamiento* (page 13) showing that you registered on the electoral register at the Town Hall is sufficient proof.

* When property is **jointly owned by a husband and wife**, both partners must be 65 years of age or over. If one is under 65, then only the person over 65 is exempt from CGT.

* **To be tax-resident** in Spain as a foreigner, you must present a certificate from the tax office showing Fiscal Resident Status: without this, the 3% retention would apply.

Residents **under the age of 65 may also qualify for relief on CGT** on sale of a home, but only if all proceeds are rolled over into purchasing another property. This option may also be exercised to a lesser degree by re-investing only part of the proceeds, in which case the exemption will apply only to that proportion of the money.

CGT on second or further properties sold by Residents is charged on the profit. This is calculated by taking the sale price then deducting from it the original purchase price, the costs and taxes involved in the acquisition, and the value when sold, as well as any profits allowable against CGT.

CGT tariffs for tax year 2011 were:

- On profit up to 6,000 Euros the tax rate is 19%
- On profit over 6,000 Euros the tax rate is 21%.

CGT for the tax years 2012 and 2013:

- On profit of up to 6,000 Euros the Tax Rate is 21%.
- On profit over 6,000 Euros and up to 24.000 Euros the Tax Rate is 25%.
- On profit over 24,000 Euros the Tax Rate is 27%.

Wealth tax and property value

Patrimonio, Wealth Tax has been raised temporarily for 2012 and 2013. These taxes will be applicable for individuals, Residents and Non-residents in Spain.

For the purposes of assessing *Patrimonio*, a property's value is understood to be the higher of: the *Valor Catastral* (rateable value); the value on the last change of ownership; or the value that the Administration has assigned to the property for any reason.

The Administration can make valuations on the following basis:

- Supplementary tax demands on the last transfer of ownership are based on the difference between the value the purchaser declared to have been paid on the *Escritura* title deed when buying and the value according to the tax authorities.
- Payment of tax on inheritance or donations of property.

Remember: If your personal assets exceed 700,000 Euros you will be liable for wealth tax for the years 2012 and 2013.

Double Taxation

Countries with which Spain has double taxation agreements on income tax include: Austria, Belgium, Brazil, Canada, Czechoslovakia, Finland, France, Germany, Holland, Hungary, Italy, Japan, Luxembourg, Morocco, Norway, Poland, Portugal, Romania, Russia, Sweden, Switzerland, Tunisia, United Kingdom, USA. These treaties applied as of April 2012.

Please note that since January 1, 2009, there has **not been a double taxation agreement with Denmark**. The Republic of **Cyprus is classed as a Fiscal Paradise**, an offshore tax haven.

The information in this book cannot be invoked as a basis for appeals. You should check the latest regulations for yourself if you are living or working across national borders. The information on taxes was prepared by Maria Jose Cobos Mayorga who is both a college registered *Gestoria Administrativa* and *Economista* where I live in Nerja, Málaga province.

The opinions expressed here and the information provided are without prejudice. It is always advisable to check all tax liabilities with a registered *Gestoria Administrativa* or *Economista* in Spain as tax laws are constantly changing.

Chapter 13: Selling Property

YOU have decided to sell your property in Spain. Maybe this is because your children have grown up and you do not need such a large property to spend holidays in; or maybe you are planning to live in Spain permanently and feel you actually need a larger property. Whatever the reason, here is what you need to know.

Many people who have been through the process agree that it is not worth the hassle of trying to sell it yourself: it is much easier to use an estate agent. If you give an agent exclusive rights to sell, they should be prepared to reduce commission rates. The flip side is that offering your property through various agents increases the possibility of getting it sold.

Agents should know market values in your area and will advise on the asking price. Another advantage of having more than one agent is that you will more likely receive a realistic valuation.

You may feel that your property is worth more than the suggested valuation. It is your call, but bear in mind that you could price yourself out of the market. Be guided by the agents, particularly in a depressed market.

The agents will take photographs of your property, put them on their web site, and display them in their office window. They will also send out details to any potential buyers and their overseas agents.

Once the agent has a buyer and a price has been agreed, they will request from the buyers a holding deposit of 3,000 Euros and a *Contrato de Reserva,* Reservation Contract, will be drawn up with the balance of the full 10% deposit being due within 15 to 21 days. This commits the purchasers to the sale, gives them time to arrange a mortgage, and allows their lawyer time to carry out necessary legal searches.

If the searches are satisfactory and/or they have an offer of a mortgage yet do not pay the balance of the 10% by the date agreed, they will lose the reservation deposit. If they go ahead as agreed, they then pay the balance of the 10% deposit and a full *Compra/Venta* purchase and sale contract will be drawn up and signed by you all.

One variation is that the agent will request the full 10% deposit on the signing of the *Compra/Venta*. This commits both parties to the Sale & Purchase of the property and the price and conditions agreed.

Whichever type of contract is signed - *Contrato de Reserva* or *CompraVenta* - a price is fixed as well as penalty clauses and the date on which final payment must be made.

The Contract will normally contain a double penalty clause stating that if the purchaser does not complete the purchase on time, they will lose the deposit to the Vendor who will then also be free to offer the property for sale to someone else.

Now listen up, because this is very important. If the Vendor does not complete on the date agreed, they have to pay the disappointed purchaser double the amount that was lodged as a deposit!

The penalty clauses ensure that both parties are locked into the contract and have entered into it having considered all the implications.

However, there is always the possibility of either the Vendor or the Purchaser being taken seriously ill just prior to the completion date of the contract. Under these circumstances it would be very harsh to impose penalties if they were unable to complete on the agreed date.

I once handled just such a situation and now suggest that a further clause is inserted to cover this eventuality. It is based on Spanish Civil Code 1.105 which states that it would not be considered as a breach of contract if delays are caused by accidents or Acts of God.

In Spanish this would read: *No supondra incumplimiento de los plazos previstos en este contrato los retrasos producidos, por caso fortuito o fuerza mayor de los recogidos en el articulo 1.105 del Codigo Civil.*

This would extend the completion date until the afflicted person was able to attend the Notary's to sign the *Escritura* title deed or a Power of Attorney was in place for somebody to sign on their behalf. For this clause to be effective there must of course be medical proof that this is the reason for invoking it and delaying completion.

The contract will also reflect the fact that the Vendor is responsible for all payments of the electricity bills, community fees, annual rates, water (if this applies) and any other encumbrances on the property up until the signing of the *Escritura.*

The Vendor is also responsible for payment of *Plus Valia* tax, which is levied by the *Ayuntamiento*, the local Town Hall, on the increase in the value of the land since it was last purchased.

Depending on how long you have had the property, the *Plus Valia* can be a considerable sum. So it is a good idea to ask either your lawyer or estate agent to obtain the figure before signing the contracts of Sale & Purchase.

When your property is sold, unless you have a valid *Residencia,* Residence Permit and can prove by way of a certificate from the Spanish tax authorities that you are paying your annual taxes as a resident in Spain, there will be a retention of 3% of the declared sale value on the *Escritura.*

If you are resident in Spain, you must obtain a certificate from the Spanish tax authorities stating that you are fiscally resident in Spain. To do this, you may have to present a certificate of *Empadronamiento* from your local *Ayuntamiento* stating that you are registered on the electoral register, as well as a copy of your NIE certificate or *Residencia.*

I suggest that you ask your *Gestoria Administrativa/Fiscal Representative* to deal with this for you, as you may well find it quite daunting to do yourself. This document must then be presented along with all the others needed at the Notary's office before you go along to sign the *Escritura.* However, do check with your lawyer/*Gestoria Administrativa* to see whether you need the tax certificate or if your *Residencia* will be sufficient to avoid having the 3% retained. If the 3% retention applies, the purchasers must deposit this with the tax authorities in Spain within one month of the signing of the *Escritura* title deed. This 3% is a deposit against your possible capital gains on the property.

Capital Gains Tax (CGT) is described more fully in Chapter 12 along with details of how you may be able to avoid paying some or any CGT. But you should anyhow ask your adviser if you can reclaim part of the 3% retention, or the total amount retained minus costs such as *Gestor's* fees.

Even if your agent has a buyer for your property, you should under no circumstances allow them possession until the *Escritura* has been signed and full and total payment has been made.

If you allow the Purchaser earlier possession, there is a danger that they may decide they do not want to buy the property but refuse to leave. You then have the problem of getting them out.

In a sticky market, your agent will maybe have someone who wants to rent your property for six months or a year, with an option to buy at the end of this period.

My advice is to refuse, as it can be fraught with danger. They may pay the rent for two months and then stop paying and refuse to leave, in which case they probably had no intention of buying in the first place.

Where does this leave you? As they have both rental and option-to-purchase contracts, it is going to take time and cost to get them out of the property. You are meanwhile unable to offer your property to anyone else until the situation is resolved. It is a worst case scenario, but it can and has happened.

If you do decide to risk agreeing to a rental and option-to-purchase contract, it is imperative that you get a lawyer to draw up the contracts. Your lawyer should ask for a substantial sum for the option-to-purchase contract. The amount paid for the option is deductible from the total selling price if the option is taken up but forfeited if not. So if the option is not taken up, you at least have some compensation for the length of time that your property has been off the market.

With regard to the final payment for your property, in my opinion the best way to deal with this is to insist that it be made by way of a Banker's Draft, made payable to you and handed over to you at the signing of the *Escritura* at the Notary's.

It may well be suggested that final payment is made by way of a transfer to your bank on the day of the signing of the *Escritura*. I would say that this is a lot more complicated and it is so much easier for both parties for it to be dealt with by Bankers Draft.

Whatever currency you are selling in, the Purchasers ask their Bank to issue them with a Banker's Draft made payable to you, and they bring it with them when they return to sign the *Escritura*.

When you put your property up for sale, if you feel you may not be able to get back to Spain for the signing of the *Escritura* to complete on the sale of your property, it makes sense to give Power of Attorney to your lawyer or somebody that you trust in Spain, to deal with it on your behalf. For full details see Chapter 6.

Whether of not you grant someone Power of Attorney, the Banker's Draft for final payment should be made payable to you then either forwarded to your address, if you want the funds in your home country, or paid into your Spanish Bank.

The estate agent or agents appointed by you to handle the sale will no doubt ask for copies of the following documents:

- A photocopy of your *Escritura* title deed.
- A photocopy of the last receipt for payment of IBI, annual rates.
- A photocopy of the last electricity bill.

- A photocopy of the last receipt of the payment of the community fees if this applies.
- A photocopy of the last water bill if this applies.
- A photocopy of the last telephone bill if this applies.
- A copy of your passport and NIE certificate

Some people are reluctant to leave a copy of their *Escritura*, but there is no need to worry about giving agents a copy as it is of no value to them.

They need either a copy of your *Escritura* or at least the land registration details because they are now obliged by law to obtain from the Land Registry a *Nota Simple*, a document showing you are the registered owners and that there are no encumbrances on your property. They also need to know the annual community fees and IBI as these costs must be included in the advertising of your property.

They will also ask you to sign a document authorising them to offer your property for sale with the price agreed as well as their commission for selling the property.

They will clearly need a set of keys for the property to be able to show prospective buyers around. If you are getting keys cut for them, please check that they will open the locks before handing them over to the agent. People have often left me keys that were so badly cut that I could not get into their properties.

When your property is sold - that is to say when a contract has been signed and a deposit has been paid - please do not forget to advise any other agents with whom you placed the property and arrange to collect the keys from them.

You would be amazed at the number of people who neglect to do this. As these other agents are unaware that the property has been sold, they may continue to show it to people, which can create somewhat embarrassing situations!

Chapter 14: General Information

NOW YOU have your property there are some aspects of looking after it and of life in Spain that will be useful to know about. I will not overload you but, hopefully, there is just enough here to make things easier as you start to settle in permanently or visit more frequently and for longer.

Security/Insurance

Insuring your property is very important, particularly when you own an apartment because, under Spanish Law, you are responsible for any damage to property below or next to you if there is a water leak or something similar. To give you some idea of insurance costs, I visited a local office of MAPFRE, one of Spain's largest insurers, just before this book was published. Depending on whether the property was a holiday home, a permanent home, and rented or not, the approximate annual insurance figures they quoted me were:

- 1 bedroom apartment, 45 square metres (m^2), contents up to 20,000 Euros, holiday home or rented out – 187 Euros.

- 1 bedroom apartment, 45 m^2, contents up to 20,000 Euros, permanent residence – 184 Euros.

- 2 bedroom apartment, 70 m^2, contents up to 20,000 Euros, holiday home or rented out - 215 Euros.

- 2 bedroom apartment, 70 m^2, contents up to 20,000 Euros, permanent residence- 208 Euros

- 2/3 bedroom townhouse, 90 m^2, contents up to 28,000 Euros, holiday home or rented out – 274 Euros.

- 2/3 bedroom townhouse, 90 m^2, contents up to 28,000 Euros, permanent residence – 263 Euros.

- 3 bedroom detached villa with pool, 120 m^2, contents up to 30,000 Euros, holiday home or rented out – 359 Euros

- 3 bedroom detached villa with pool, 120 m^2, contents up to 30,000 Euros, permanent residence – 342 Euros

Check that insurance is valid if the property is not being used for long periods, and whether you have to advise the insurers if it is being left empty for any length of time. The insurance agent may ask if the windows have *rejas,* iron bars, and if there is an alarm system, which should reduce the premiums. They will also need a separate list of items of value such as jewellery, as normal insurance would not cover these.

Before signing the agreement, ensure that you understand fully what is and what is not covered by the policy. Normal policies cover Acts of God (such as lightning, flooding etc) as well as robbery, but many will limit the amount insured. For example, your cover may be quite restricted if rainfall of more than 40 litres per square metre is recorded, winds of over 90 kilometres per hour, of if there is hail and snow. Check the fine print!

You should certainly have no problem getting insurance. Ask for recommendations from the agent you bought your property from and/or speak to other foreigners who have already purchased property in the area that you are buying in.

Renting out property

If you are not living permanently in Spain, you may want to rent out your home when you are not using it, to recover some costs. There is no shortage of agencies that would be more than happy to rent your property. They generally take between 10% and 20% of the rent as commission and deal not only with the renting but also with cleaning and the laundering of bed linen. They charge separately for cleaning, laundry, gas cylinders and any other costs that they may incur.

The agency should issue an annual statement of your account, showing rental income and expenses. A good idea is to ask people you know who already rent out their properties if they can recommend a particular agency.

Estate agents will very often offer a rental/management service as well, but if the agent your are buying from does not deal with rentals, they should be able to recommend someone. Cowboy agencies, the disreputable ones, are to be avoided at all costs. So, be sure to get a solid recommendation before you enter into anything.

I asked a long established and reputable estate agent where I live in Nerja. Málaga, and with which I have dealt for many years, to give me some idea of what owners expect from renting out property and what potential renters expect. Their replies give an idea of services and charges that you might expect or even demand from similarly well-run letting agencies.

What Owners Want

Owners want the highest rental income with the lowest costs and least hassle. The rental agent I spoke to takes 20% commission and shares it 50:50 with its collaborators around the world so they can source bookings all year round rather than being reliant on any particular school holiday season.

They charge owners only when the agency actually does anything, for example a fee for securing a rental, a cleaning charge when they clean, a laundry charge when they change the laundry, a pool maintenance charge per visit, a gardening charge per visit. This way there is complete transparency on fees.

They do not believe in yearly or monthly management charges, or key-holding charges, as they believe this can sometimes be difficult to substantiate, particularly if the property in question has not rented well. If they do rent the property on their books they would naturally hold the keys, so why make a charge?

Like many of the better agents that have weathered the property downturn, this rental agent has 'inherited' a large number of property owners due to previous bad experiences of what they refer to internally as 'mama and papa agents' who conduct their business from either their home or the local bar. The most frequent complaints about bad agents is that the owners never know if their property is being rented out or not, they do not know what rent is being charged so have no idea what they are due, and they sometimes suspect that they are maybe not told about all the rentals that have been made.

This same rental agent has invested heavily in an automated booking system that sends notification to property owners the second that the agent takes the booking. So owners know at all times if the property is occupied or not. They do not pay owners in a bar, in cash, but produce official invoices with IVA (value added tax) applied and transfer money into owners' bank accounts. Their entire rental team is employed, registered and insured. So everything is above board and on the right side of Spanish tax and accounting rules for the sake of both owners and the agency. They can also show owners the projected and actual percentages of occupancy, so owners can predict yield.

They do not call 'a mate who knows a mate' to fix electrical faults, they send their own qualified electrician and receive a report which is passed on to owners. They do not ask a neighbour to do 'a quick clean' but instead have a professional cleaning team equipped with smart phones so they can also check inventories and report damage as well as sending photos to back up reports. This allows them to debit a holidaymaker's credit card as per terms and conditions to replace or repair whatever was damaged.

They do not accept the notion that it is just bad luck when something breaks. They fix it, again supported by photos, to show owners.

What Holidaymakers Want

High profile frauds have made some holidaymakers nervous about booking properties in Spain by internet. Unsuspecting holidaymakers have made reservations and payment online only to discover on reaching the resort that neither the agent nor the property exist.

Rental agents tell me they are often asked: How do I know you exist? How do I know the property is yours to rent? How do I know my money is not just going in to your back pocket?

Having a physical presence benefits the agency as holidaymakers already in the resort can visit their offices maybe seven days a week, 365 days a year, or call them around the clock for help and advice. The result is that they have been getting 58% repeat business, high by industry standards. Holidaymakers feel safer with a completely legal, fully registered and insured agent in the centre of town and available around the clock!

If you decide not to rent out, but would like **someone to keep an eye on your property** while you are not in Spain, look for a reliable agency or ask the locals if they can recommend someone to give you a management contract which at the very least should include: a weekly visit; airing the property; watering plants; and checking for damp and water leaks before any serious damage is done. I personally believe that it is worthwhile.

To provide an idea of the **cost of a management only contract**, I asked a local agency which quoted the following approximate annual figures: 250 Euros for a one bedroom property; 300 Euros for a two bedroom property; and 350 Euros for a three bedroom property.

Management costs may well be minimal if the contractor is also renting the property for you. They would be checking it anyhow when it is rented, so a management charge should only apply if the property was empty for a reasonable period.

Parking and vehicle purchase

I have always been aware of, and often exasperated by, the lack of information about parking restrictions. Spanish authorities seem to delight in towing away cars then slapping on hefty fines to retrieve them from the pound. Often the 'culprit' is none the wiser for his misdeed. So this is an attempt to make life a little easier for tourists and non-Spanish speaking residents:

No Parking: Red border ring, red X on a blue background. Normally on a metal pole at the edge of the kerb, or against the wall if it is a pathway.

Stop only for a few minutes: Red border ring, single red diagonal line on a navy blue background.

Pay and display: Square sign on a pole, white background with red border ring and a single red diagonal line on a navy blue background. Look for the ticket machine where you pay. Leave the ticket visible in car.

No parking this side of road from 1-15 or 16-31 of month: Red border ring, single red diagonal line on a navy blue background with 1-15 written in white. On the opposite side of the road there will be an identical sign but with the dates 16-31. As above but the box underneath, in white with a black border and the writing in black on a white background, states **MES IMPAR** (the side of the street with odd numbers) which means there is No Parking on this side of the road in the months of Enero (January), Marzo (March), Mayo (May), Julio (July), Septiembre (September) and Noviembre (November). On the other side of the road there will be the same sign stating **MES PAR** (the side of the street with even numbers) which means there is No Parking in Febrero (February), Abril (April), Junio (June), Agosto (August), Octubre (October) and Diciembre (December).

Other parking restrictions: You might find a yellow line painted on the edge of the kerb, with a sign similar to the No Parking type, and bearing one diagonal line and the words **Excepto Carga y Descarga 8h a 14h.** This means that you cannot park during the hours of 08.00 to 14.00 because this is a loading and unloading area. You are, however, allowed to park *before* and *after* these times.

Key point: If in doubt, park where there are no signs: being taken away by the *grua* tow truck is very costly!

Traffic Department - *Trafico*

The Traffic Department's procedures are complex, and you are strongly recommended to use a *Gestoria Administrativa* to deal with them for you. However, if you prefer, you may do it yourself.

Buying a Car

To buy a car in Spain you will need to present the following documentation:

• A certificate of your registration on the electoral register *(Certificado de Empadronamiento)* from the local *Ayuntamiento*, Town Hall.

• A rental contract for an apartment/house for a minimum of one year or an *Escritura* title deed, or a valid *Residencia*.

New Cars

The car dealer will normally register the vehicle in your name at a cost of approximately 300 Euros, but you also have to pay a registration tax, which varies according to engine size the price of the car.

Used Cars

When buying a second hand car you need the following documents so your *Gestoria Administrativa* can transfer the vehicle to your name:

• The *Inspeccion Tecnica de Vehiculos card,* which is the vehicle log book, as well as a current ITV certificate, equivalent to 'the MOT' in the UK.

• The *Permiso de Circulacion,* a white registration card, which must be signed by the seller of the vehicle to authorise the transfer to your name.

• A certificate from the *Recaudacion Provincial* rates office showing there are no outstanding *Impuestos de Circulacion* annual road tax payments or fines.

Contract of Sale

This contract can be made by the interested party and it will have to show the following:

- The buyer's and seller's names and addresses and the identification number from their valid passport and their *NIE/Residencia* or *DNI*.
- The vehicle model and registration number
- Sale price
- Form of payment
- That the vehicle is free of charges
- Date of contract
- Signatures of buyer and seller

The seller, buyer or their *Gestor* will have to present the original contract and a photocopy, along with copies of passports and NIE certificate or *Residencia* in the case of foreign sellers/buyers, or their DNI (document of identification) if they are Spanish, to the *Trafico* office that will stamp the copy presented. At this point, the seller will be exempt of any responsibility for fines, accidents or traffic taxes in subsequent years.

The seller or their Gestor should then present this stamped copy to the Town Hall's *Rentas* Department so that no future requests for payment of the Vehicle Tax are made to him or her.

Things you need to know as a seller

Transfer of Previous Title to the New Owner: Responsibility for the transfer of a car or motorbike is **the responsibility of the seller not the buyer**, and it is most important that this is dealt with **before handing over the vehicle**.

To avoid unnecessary journeys and having to make the appropriate transactions in the offices of *Trafico*, I advise asking a *Gestoria Administrativa* to deal with this on your behalf. The *Gestoria*

Administrativa's fees are approximately 60 Euros plus IVA (VAT). You could do this yourself, but dealing with *Trafico* can be a nightmare.

It is very important that the vehicle that you are selling is transferred to the name of the buyer. Otherwise, road tax and fines will continue to be sent out in your name and you will be responsible for these payments until ownership is transferred officially. Therefore the seller of the vehicle should pay the *Gestor's* fees for dealing with the transfer, ensuring that this is done.

The transfer tax depends on the age and the cylinder capacity of the vehicle. As a guide, a five year old Opel Corsa would be approximately 180 Euros and a two year old motorcycle of 250cc some 114 Euros.

To transfer the vehicle to a buyer's name you need the following:

- Photocopy of buyer's passport, NIE/ *Residencia* certificate or DNI, proof of address, i.e. *Escritura*, rental contract or *Certificado de Empadronamiento*.
- Photocopy of seller's passport, NIE/ *Residencia* certificate or DNI.
- The transfer document signed by both parties
- The *Tarjeta de Inspeccion Tecnica*, Technical Inspection Card, showing that the vehicle has a current ITV (MOT in the UK) certificate
- The *Permiso de Circulacion* white circulation card

So your car was sold but you still get demands for tax! This very likely means that the transfer was never carried out, so you are still registered as the owner and are responsible for any tax, fines or accident expenses.

Options to resolve this include:

1. Pay all outstanding taxes at the *Oficina de Recaudacion* tax office

and de-register the vehicle at the *Trafico* offices, presenting the last paid receipt. Then present a copy of the de-registration to the Town Hall's *Rentas* Department to annul future vehicle receipts.

2. If your car was not sold, but you no longer possess either the vehicle or the documents, you must go to the Town Hall's *Rentas* Department to cancel the Road Tax demands. If you are still receiving demands for road tax, or possibly fines, contact your *Gestoria Administrativa* immediately and ask to get the car cancelled on the *Trafico* computer system. Until this is dealt with you are liable for these debts, and interest charges will be added on a daily basis. Bank accounts may also be embargoed until such time as payment is made.

Buying a motorcycle or moped

New

More than 49 cc: Same as for a car.
Up to 49 cc: Once purchased, get the registration from *Trafico*. This is often dealt with by the dealer.

Second hand

More than 49 cc: Same as for a car.
Up to 49 cc: Deal with the transfer of ownership at *Trafico*. Better to ask a *Gestoria Administrativa* about documents and cost.

ITV Technical Inspection of Vehicles

All cars, vans, mopeds and motorbikes must be inspected periodically. It is illegal to buy, sell or insure a vehicle lacking a current ITV certificate. At the ITV test centre you must present the *Permiso de Circulacion,* which is the white coloured Circulation Permit, and the *Tarjeta de Inspeccion Tecnica de Vehiculos* Technical Inspection Card.

Cars

A **new car** must be inspected after **four** years. A car of **four to ten years** must be inspected every **two** years. A car of **more than ten years** must be inspected **annually**. Recently, ITV charges were nearly **37 Euros for a petrol car** and **42 Euros for a diesel car.**

Vans

New vans must be inspected **after two years.** Vans of **more than six years** must go through the ITV **annually.** Vans **over ten years** old must be inspected **every six months.** Recently, ITV charges were nearly **40 Euros for a petrol van** and **45 Euros for a diesel one.**

Mopeds up to 49 cc

A new moped or motorbike of up to 49 cc is inspected after three years at a cost of nearly 22 Euros for the former and almost 33 Euros for the latter.

Motorcycles or scooters of more than 49 cc

A new motorbike or moped/scooter of more than 49 cc is inspected after three years at a cost of nearly 33 Euros for either.

Notes on costs: Costs quoted for ITV are a guide. These figures were for Andalucía, the Southern region of Spain, and can vary from one province to another.

Vehicles with foreign registration

A car with a foreign registration can stay in Spain for **only six months** in any calendar year. Beyond this, the car must be taken out of Spain or must be re-registered with a Spanish plate. It is possible to request an **extension of six months** if the owner can prove sufficient economic means for that period.

Importing a foreign registered car and changing to Spanish registration

This is a complex procedure best handled by a *Gestoria Administrativa*. Fees for this will be approximately 300 Euros as well as charges made by *Trafico* for the *Certificado Tecnica*, the *Impuestos de Circulacion* road tax, and the *Matricula* registration number plate.

The cost of all this documentation is around 400 Euros in addition to the *Gestor's* fees. You take these documents and the number plate along with the vehicle to have an ITV (the equivalent of a UK MOT) costing about **110** to **130** Euros.

High import taxes and registration costs mean that —unless your vehicle is virtually new - my advice is to sell before you leave your country and then purchase a car in Spain. Apart from the cost of importing, if the vehicle is a right-hand drive car it will bring its own problems when trying to overtake on single carriage roads, while the headlights will also have to be adjusted for driving on the right hand side of the road.

Road taxes - *Impuestos de Circulacion:*

Anyone owning a vehicle is subject to this tax. For example, the **annual tariffs** where I live are approximately as follows but will vary elsewhere:

Cars

Up to 7.99 Horse Power (HP): 22.20 Euros
From 8HP to 11.99 HP: 60.10 Euros
From 13HP to 15.99: 134.30 Euros
From 16HP to 19.99 HP: 167.30 Euros
19.99 HP to 1,000 HP: 209.10 Euros

Mopeds

7.66 Euros

Motorcycles

Up to 125cc: 7.80 Euros
126cc to 250cc: 13.40 Euros
251cc to 500cc: 26.70 Euros
501cc to 1,000cc: 53.40 Euros
more than 1,000cc: 106.80 Euros

Garage entrance - *Entrada de Vehiculos:*

Anyone who owns a garage or an entrance, such as gates, from the roadway giving vehicle access to a house or a building is subject to this tax. For illustration, my **local annual tariffs** in 2012 depend on whether they apply to an individual or communal garage and are approximately:

Individual garage
Up to 3 metres of frontage: 83 Euros
Each metre of additional frontage: 18.03 Euros

Communal garage
For garages each up to 3 metres of frontage:
- With 2 parking places 51.20 Euros for each parking place
- With 3 parking places: 34.40 Euros each
- With 4 parking places: 25.60 Euros each
- With 5 or more: 20.70 Euros each
- For each metre of additional frontage, shared proportionally among the garages: 30.70 Euros each

Each vehicle entrance must display a *Vado Permanente* sign (entrance permanently in use) so that people do not park in front of it. Then if a vehicle obstructs the entrance, you can call the tow truck *(grua)* to take the vehicle away. Where I live, this sign costs about 46.10 Euros. It is payable only once and should be requested at the *Rentas* Department of the Town Hall.

Local variations: In Spain, each Town Hall sets its own Road Tax and Garage Entrance Tax. So the figures quoted are for Nerja, Málaga, where I live, and could vary tremendously in other towns and villages.

Building permits - *Licencias de Construccion*

Permission is needed for any building work in or outside property. For example, if you want to re-tile a bathroom or terrace, or to replace windows, you need a licence from the local Town Hall. Go to the *Departamento de Urbanismo,* planning department, and fill in a form requesting a licence for *Obra Menor,* minor building work, with the address of your property, the work planned, and the cost. The price of the licence is fairly low, but if you do not get permission fines can be quite high.

If you want to build something more ambitious, say an extension to add another bedroom, check with the *Departamento de Urbanismo* to see if they will give you permission. If so, you present architect's plans, building costs and the address. A building licence for works of this type costs much more than for minor work or refurbishing.

You may also need authorisation from your community of owners to carry out building work on the inside or outside of your property.

The budget that you present should include the price of the materials and the labour costs, the cost of electricity, carpentry and suchlike: even if the work is to be carried out by the owner this must be quoted at a professional rate.

Requesting a Permit

All works must have a licence before commencement. This may be requested by: the owner of the house; a representative of the owner; or the builder.

If you cannot present the application personally, you would need to give your representative or the builder a notarised *Poder Notarial,* Power of Attorney, to do so on your behalf. The cost of the *Poder Notarial,* if it is made in Spain, would be approximately 65 Euros. If the Power of Attorney is made outside of Spain, the cost could be considerably higher and must be in a bilingual Spanish/own language format with an *Apostille* attached to legalise it for use in Spain (Chapter 6).

Alterations to existing buildings are considered to be **Obra Menor**, small work. For example:

- Re-tiling floors
- Re-tiling kitchen or bathroom walls
- Building or removing interior partitions
- Re-placing or removing doors, windows, gratings
- Tiling a garden or terrace
- Decorative girders/pergolas for garden or terrace
- Raising garden walls

Such works do not need plans, and after payment the permit is normally granted within a couple of weeks.

Licence charges for *Obra Menor* (small building works)

Where I live – and it may well be different where you are - the cost of the licence for small building work is 7.1% up to a value of 60,000 Euros, above which it becomes 7.6%. The licence is paid in two parts: 3.3% on applying for it, and the rest when the licence is issued. If the work is valued at more than 60,000 Euros, 3.8% is paid on application and the balance when the licence is issued. There is a minimum charge of 31.10 Euros. As I say, this is where I live. Check your own Town Hall or ask your adviser to do this for you before launching any work.

Licence charges for *Obra Mayor* (large building works)

The extension or construction of a new house is considered *Obra Mayor,* large work. For example:

- Building a new house
- Extensions, roofs, garages
- An additional floor/storey
- Roofing over a terrace or garden

These works need plans approved by the College of Architects. The **architect's fees** vary around 5% to 10% of the value of the work and **do not** include the cost of the building permit. The cost of the *Licencia de Obra Mayor* in Nerja, where I live, is currently 7.6% of the building quotation.

Requirements for carrying out any work

The Building Permit is granted by the Town Hall only if:
- The house is in a legal urbanisation or approved building zone
- The square meterage complies with building regulations
- It is approved by the planning department

Completed work will be surveyed by the architect's office in the Town Hall. If they deem the value of work carried out to be higher than the amount declared when the licence was applied for, then you will have to pay a proportionately higher licence fee than you expected.

Occupation of Public Way with construction materials

If a skip, materials, rubble or other waste spills on to the pavement or road, you will receive, on completion, a notice to pay a Public Way Occupation Tax, which in my town is 0.80 Euros per metre per day depending on location.

Planning Breaches

If you do not request a licence, or what was built does not correspond with what was applied for, you will have breached planning and will be subject to **a fine and possibly a demolition order.**

Where I live, this fine is between 1 % and 5% of the budget of the work if it is possible to legalise the construction; and between 10% and 20% if it is impossible, in which case demolition proceedings will be initiated. Aside from the fine, you have to pay the building licence of the completed works, which will be evaluated by technical personnel of the Town Hall.

Recommended action

Before starting work, get a written quotation from the builder itemising what will be done and the quality of the materials –i.e. the type and cost of tiles for walls and floors, doors, windows, etc. The budget should include:

- Details of the company that will do the works
- The owner's name and the address of the property
- Description of projects with price of labour and materials
- Total price including taxes
- Completion date
- Date and signature of builder or professional
- Date and signature of applicant
- Guarantee
- Form of payment

The builder should not charge for estimates. The constructor is responsible for any damage that he or his workers cause to the dwelling or to other persons or dwelling during work.

Payment of local taxes

When: All receipts are annual. *Impuestos de Circulacion*, Road Tax, is normally paid from March to May and IBI, popularly known as *'Contribuciones'*, from June to September. The time to pay may vary from year to year. From the date on the invoice, you have around three months to pay.

Where and how: There are two options.

By Banker's Standing Order: This is the most effective way since it avoids surcharges and having to find out when a given invoice is due for payment. You fill in an authorisation in the *Oficina de Recaudacion Provincial*, Rates Office, where they give you two copies: one to give to your bank and the other to keep. You cannot make a standing order for annual rates if there are outstanding bills from previous years.

At the Bank: If the IBI is not paid by direct debit you will have to go to one of the banks listed on the notification that you will receive by post to your Spanish address (not your home country's address). If for any reason you do not receive this notification, go to your local *Recaudacion Provincial* office to get this bill and pay at one of the banks indicated.

Unpaid Road Tax or IBI

Invoices that go unpaid within the prescribed dates will attract a 20% surcharge plus interest, and will also have the costs of legal action added if it is taken. If payment is not made by a certain date, the Tax Collection Office will proceed to embargo bank accounts and then the property.

Census Register - *Empadronamiento*

The census is the official record of inhabitants registered at the Town Hall. It is also used to create the electoral census of persons aged over 18 who have the right to vote in elections. The census is of great importance as the registered number of inhabitants determines how much the local area gets from central and regional government towards the cost of: municipal services such as local police, refuse, water, sewerage, street lighting, local roads; and state services such as national police, doctors, hospitals, colleges, civil guard, highways, and courts. If you do not register, you will generally be viewed as someone who is cheating your city, town or village out of the money it needs to pay for the services you are getting.

All persons who normally reside in a municipality are **obliged to**

register with the Town Hall. People residing in several localities must register in the place where they reside for the greatest length of time. A person may not be registered in two or more municipalities at the same time. A person wishing to live in another municipality has to request from the Town Hall a document showing his removal from the census and then present this to the Town Hall of the new municipality where he is going to live. Registration on the Census is free and can be done at any time of the year.

Requirements for registration

All foreigners with *Residencia,* Residence permits, are obliged to register, as must all Spanish residents. Present a copy of your *Residencia* at the *Oficina de Empadronamiento,* Census Department, in the Town Hall. However, you do not need to have *Residencia* in Spain to join the electoral register. As long as you own or are renting a property in the area, you can register. Simply present your passport and a copy of your *Escritura* title deeds, or a rental contract, to prove that you have permanent residence in Spain. As requirements may vary from province to province you should check with your Town Hall regarding documentation.

Advantages of being registered

People who are registered may: stand for **election or vote** in local and European Parliament elections. Currently though, foreigners cannot stand for or vote in Spanish Regional or National elections; request **cohabitation, residence and registration certificates**, which are needed for: collecting unemployment and pension payments, requesting medical assistance in the Outpatients Department of the Social Security Hospital; and for various procedures with the Administration; **buy a car as a foreigner**; and be a member of a Town Hall provided *Hogar de Pensionistas,* **Pensioners' Club**, which has financial and social benefits.

National Census

This happens every five years when the government employs enumerators to call at homes with census forms that must be filled in for every member of the household. If they do not visit you, you must go to the Census Department of the Town Hall and provide the necessary information.

If you were registered in the previous National census and your information has not been taken when the new census is being checked, you will be excluded.

Foreigners whose *Residencia* has expired and who within six months have not presented an up to date *Residencia* to the Census Department at the Town Hall will also be excluded.

Checking that you are registered

Go to the *Oficina de Empadronamiento* at the Town Hall. This is essential at election time: if you are not on the census, or there are mistakes in your data, you will not be able to vote. Changes of address must also be notified to this Department.

Water

Once you buy property, transfer the water meter to your name. My water board charges for this: currently 125 Euros for a 15mm meter and 150 Euros for a 30mm one. It also takes a deposit of 95 Euros for the meter, a sum returned on sale of the property. Costs vary by area, so ask your lawyer or estate agent.

When you buy new property from a developer who should have installed a water meter, you need a document called a *boletin* from him to prove that an approved plumber installed the plumbing. If you need to replace the existing water meter – maybe it is faulty - the water board will charge around 400 Euros including IVA value added tax. Any modifications needed to install a new water meter will add to costs.

To have a water meter registered in your name for a new property, or to transfer an existing meter to your name, you need:

- For a new build property: the *boletin* of installation and a photocopy of your *Escritura* title deed
- For a resale property: photocopies of your *Escritura* and the water bill from the previous owners
- A photocopy of your NIE or *Residencia*
- Your bank account details to set up a standing order
- In some areas of Spain, they may ask for a certificate from either the Town Hall or the *Recaudacion Provincial* rates office showing you owe nothing to local authorities

Paying for water use

Water is not expensive despite lack of rainfall in many areas. The minimum charge if no water is used during the quarter and for either a 15mm or 30mm meter is eight Euros where I live but can vary elsewhere.

For me, the cost of water per cubic metre (m^3) consumed is:

- Up to 20 m^3 ~ 0.23 Euros plus IVA
- 21 to 40 m^3 ~ 0.48 Euros plus IVA
- 41 to 80 m^3 ~0.68 Euros plus IVA

Disconnection of water because of non-payment

Payment is due within a month of the invoice date, after which the Water Company sends a demand by registered letter. If payment is not made within 15 days of the demand, the water will be cut off. The cost of reconnection is around 39 Euros for a 15mm meter and 118 Euros for a 30mm one, on top of the outstanding debt.

Electricity

Resale Property

To transfer the electricity contract to your name/s, present these documents to a power company's local offices:

- A photocopy of the *Escritura* title deed
- A photocopy of your NIE certificate or *Residencia*
- Your bank account details for a standing order
- A copy of an electric bill from the previous owners
- The *Boletin* of the installation (see below)

Please note that you should ask your lawyer or estate agent to contact the electricity company supplying the owners that you are buying from to see if you will need two things done to allow the supply to be transferred to your name. These could be a new trip-switch system and/or the replacement of wiring to the electric meter. If so, you will need an approved electrician to do the work who will then give you a *Boletin de Instalacion,* a certificate confirming the necessary changes have been carried out and by an authorised professional.

This can cost around **600 Euros** to **1,500 Euros** depending on the work, hence the reason for asking your lawyer or estate agent to see if it is necessary.

When you, your lawyer, or your estate agent go to the electricity company, the supplier will ask for a contact telephone number for someone who can let them in to the property so they can send a technician to check the system and to install an ICP, a circuit breaker to stop you drawing more power than you have contracted for.

This technician will normally call a few days after you have presented all the relevant documents at the electricity offices. There is a charge of approximately **32 Euros** to transfer the electricity contract to your name.

New Property

To get a meter, present these documents at the electricity company's local offices:

- A photocopy of the *Escritura* title deed
- A photocopy of your NIE certificate or *Residencia*
- Your bank account details for a standing order
- The B*oletin* of the installation, given to you by the developer/builder
- A photocopy of the *Licencia de Primera Ocupacion* from the planning department at the Town Hall, which should be given to you by the developer/builder

The charge for installing the electricity meter will be around **155 Euros** for a meter rated at 4.06 kilowatts (kW) and **200 Euros** for one of 5.75 kW. The electricity company will send the bill for installation to your bank for payment.

Tariff

When you apply for the electricity meter you may contract up to the maximum kWs approved on the *Boletin de Instalacion*. The more kWs contracted, the higher the standing charge you pay whether the house is inhabited or empty. As a rough guide, a contract for 4.4 kW will mean a **standing charge** of 7.50 Euros every month plus the amount of power used.

Disconnection of electricity because of non-payment

Electricity bills need paying within 15 days, after which you receive a demand notice by registered letter. If payment is not made within 15 days of the demand notice, the supply will be cut off. The reconnection charge is around 38 Euros on top of the outstanding debt.

If you set up a standing order for electricity bills, there should be no danger of disconnection. However, Spanish banks cannot give you an overdraft if you are not resident in Spain. So if your bill is for 75 Euros and you have only 74 Euros in your account, they cannot legally pay regardless of how good a client you may be. So you must **always ensure that you have sufficient funds in your Spanish account**.

Telephone

Applying for a telephone

There is intense competition to provide fixed and mobile telephone services in Spain, but Telefónica, operating as Movistar, is the provider of lines and one of the more dependable suppliers of call packages.

By all means shop around. Vodafone, Jazztel and Yoigo are other significant providers, and many companies allow you to sign up online too. But let us assume that you choose *Movistar*. Go to the nearest *Movistar* office or ring freephone number 1004 to apply for a line. You can also ask for someone speaks English if you wish.

You may ring *Movistar* from a call box or from a mobile. But if you use a mobile, your call may go to the main offices in Madrid whereas you really need to speak to an operator in the province where you want the phone line connected.

When applying, you will need to provide your passport or NIE number, your full name and address in Spain, your bank details and name of your bank, and the twenty digits which are on the top right-hand corner of your Spanish chequebook.

If you apply for your telephone at a *Movistar* office in the town where you are buying property, you will need the following documents:

- A photocopy of your Passport or your *Residencia* or NIE certificate
- A photocopy of your *Escritura* title deed or a rental contract for the property where you want the telephone
- Your bank details.

Tariffs

These are rounded examples of what *Movistar* was charging for installation at one point going into 2012:

- Installing a digital telephone line 175 Euros plus IVA Installing an analogue line 34 Euros plus IVA
- ADSL broadband installation 38 Euros plus IVA

Standing charges

Movistar applies a standing charge every month for the use of the line and regardless of how many calls were made. In early 2012, the standing charge per month was around 13 Euros including IVA.

Reduced call charges

Calls within Spain are at a reduced tariff on: Monday to Friday from 22.00 hours to 08:00 hours; Saturdays from 14:00; and all day Sundays and holidays.

International telephone calls are at a reduced tariff overnight Monday to Saturday from 22.00 hours until 08.00 hours, all day Sunday, and on National Holidays.

Disconnection because of non-payment

The telephone is cut off 20 days after non-payment of the invoice. Recently, the reconnection charge was roughly 15 Euros plus the outstanding bill. The line is normally reconnected within 48 hours of payment.

Making telephone calls

To Spanish provinces: Dial the prefix for each province before the individual phone number.

International calls: Dial as follows:

- 00 (to signify an international number)
- The number of the country (United Kingdom is 44; France 33; Germany 49; Norway 47; Sweden 46, etc)
- The prefix of the town or city but without the zero at the start of the area code. So 0207 for central London becomes just 207
- The number of the subscriber

Doctors

Tariffs for private consultations: Where I live, charges for private medical consultations vary between 30 Euros and 60 Euros. Medical assistance at home ranges between 50 Euros and 120 Euros. A consultation with a basic blood analysis costs approximately 50 Euros. Medical invoices should not include IVA, value added tax

Banks

Hours of opening to the public are generally:

- Monday to Friday 08:30 to 14:00
- Saturdays 08.30 to 14.00 (but only in winter and not all branches or locations, and not savings banks)
- Local holidays: closed
- National holidays: closed

There has recently been more variation in opening hours depending on the bank, the branch, and the type of location. Some banks now extend opening hours at key points in the month when many people will be paying tax or IVA.

Opening an account: Anyone aged 18 or older can open a bank account. Just present your passports and a copy of your NIE certificates, giving your permanent address in your home country for correspondence if you are not living in Spain, and pay in a small amount to activate the account. If you wish, you may also open an account in foreign currencies. All except Non Residents' accounts are subject to the withholding for tax of 25% of any interest earned.

Schools

As more people decide to live and work in Spain, I am constantly asked about schools.

If you decide to place your child in a **Spanish state school**, the enrolment period is normally during April. Go to the school of your choice, which would logically be nearest to where you are living, and ask for an application form. You will have to give a second or third choice school as there may be insufficient places available in the school of your choice.

To register your child, you need to prove you are resident in Spain and present a copy of your *Residencia* and *Empadronamiento* (Certificate of Registration on the Electoral Register) from the local Town Hall *(Ayuntamiento)*. To obtain this certificate, go to your local Town Hall to the *Oficina de Empadronamiento,* Electoral Registry office, and register. This will involve showing your passport or *Residencia* as well as a rental contract or a copy of your *Escritura title* deed as proof that you are living permanently in the Town or Village.

If you arrive outside of the enrolment period, you need to check with local schools to see if it is possible to admit children at that time. You cannot take it for granted.

There are nursery schools for children from age three. Infant school normally starts at the age of 4 to 5 years, junior school at six through to 12, and secondary/senior school from 12 to 16. The school year for infants and juniors normally starts around September 15, and a week later for Secondary/Senior school.

At the end of June, schools publish lists of books required, and which you have to buy, for the next year's courses. The list is posted on a notice board at the school.

If you prefer your children to have a **private education**, there are

English speaking International schools all around the coast of Spain and in some major inland cities including Madrid. The cost of going private varies tremendously, so check in the area where you are buying to see what private schools are available and what they charge.

If your children are still quite young, one advantage of a Spanish state school is that, after an initial struggle, they will soon pick up Spanish and end up speaking it like a native, which helps them to fit in. Some parents put children into a state school until 12 years of age and then transfer them to a private school.

You should also be aware that private schools are not obliged to take your children. Some headmasters of these schools complain that parents who have not thought things through in advance sometimes resort to moral blackmail to force their children on schools even though class sizes may be at their limit and other pupils could suffer as a result.

Taking your Pets

It is now relatively simple to take your dog, cat, or any other pet into Spain provided you have the relevant documentation in advance. You need a European Union (EU) pet's passport from your local vet. To get this, your pet must have a rabies injection and have an identification microchip inserted. Organise the pet passport well in advance in case there are delays. If you are moving from the United Kingdom and your local vet cannot help, or if you have any questions, ring the UK Department for Environment, Food & Rural Affairs (DEFRA) helpline at 08459 335577 or go to the website www.defra.gov.uk

Taking a horse to Spain is more complicated than for pets. Contact DEFRA or its equivalent in your own country for advice. **If you decide** to sell up in Spain and return with your pet to the UK, as from January 1, 2012, DEFRA's regulations for taking a pet into the UK are as follows: To avoid quarantine you will need to have your pet microchipped before any of the other procedures for pet travel are carried out. After the microchip has been fitted, your pet must be vaccinated against rabies. There is no exemption to this requirement, even if you pet has a current rabies vaccination. Rabies boosters must be kept up to date. The length of the waiting period before entry to the U.K. is 21 days after the first vaccination date. A waiting period is not required for subsequent entries into the U.K., provided rabies boosters are kept up to date. If the vaccination is in two parts the 21day waiting period will be from the date of the second vaccination. For animals being prepared in an EU country, you should get an EU pet passport. Please note that although Gibraltar is not an EU country, they can issue a pet passport for pets being returned to the UK.

Tapeworm treatment: DEFRA expects the European Commission to shortly come forward with proposals to allow the UK to still require pets to be treated against tapeworm. The pet must be treated against tapeworm 24 to 48 hours prior to travelling, and issued with an official certificate of treatment. There will be no mandatory requirements for tick treatment. Regulations change. So ring the DEFRA helpline or check www.defra.gov.uk for the latest official rules.

If you are selling your property and returning to a country other than the UK, you will need to check with your own authorities.

I know a company, Airpets Oceanic (APO), that has specialised in shipping pets abroad from the UK for some 40 years. They are registered with IPATA, the International Pet & Animal Transportation Association. APO deals with everything from booking flights, handling veterinary documentation, collecting pets and keeping them comfortably at their kennels for as long as needed, and arranging for pets to be collected at the airport and delivered to your new home.

Air Pets Oceanic appears to offer a very complete service, so if you are planning to take your pets to Spain from the United Kingdom, check them out. They are based at Spout Lane North, Stanwell Moor, Staines, Middlesex TW19 6BW, United Kingdom - tel +44 (0)1753 685571, Freephone 0800-371554, email **info@airpets.co.uk** but website **www.airpets.com**

National Holidays

Spaniards work hard and love to let their hair down with family and friends on the many local and national holidays that punctuate the year.

The local holidays will usually be listed on your Town Hall website or can be got from their offices. National holidays are:

January 1: New Year
January 6: Epiphany
March or April: Easter
May 1: May Day
August 15: The Feast of the Assumption
October 12: Spain Day
November 1: All Saints' Day
December 6: Constitution Day
December 8: The Feast of the Immaculate Conception
December 25: Christmas Day

Note: If a National holiday falls on a Sunday, the holiday will be celebrated on the following Monday. Sometimes, if a national holiday leaves only one working day before the next day off, maybe a Sunday or another holiday, post offices, some public offices, banks, shops and other businesses may also be closed on the intervening work day, a custom known as taking a 'puente', a bridge. For example, if May Day is on a Thursday, some businesses may also be closed on the 'bridge day', Friday, so that employees get a long weekend off.

The government is now talking of stopping the practice of the puente by changing holidays that fall during the working week to a Friday or Monday. My advice meanwhile is not to seethe with indignation but to go with the flow and enjoy the party. When in Spain, do as the Spanish do!

Appendix A: Property Transfer Taxes 2012

Each region of Spain sets its own transfer taxes on property sales (*Impuestos Sobre Transmisiones Patrimoniales*). In 2012, these were :

Andalucía

- For an apartment, villa, townhouse , farmhouse, and including commercial premises, the taxes for various declared sales values are::
    - Up to 400,000 Euros – 8%
    - 401,000 to 700,000 Euros – 9%
    - 701,000 Euros and more – 10%
- A garage or a parking space, both beneath an apartment block and valued at up to 30,000 Euros – 8%
- The same garage or parking space valued at 30,001 to 50,000 Euros – 9%

Asturias

- Up to 300,000 Euros – 8%
- 300,001 to 500,00 Euros – 9%
- more than 500,000 Euros – 10%

Cantabria

- Up to 300,000 Euros – 7%
- More than 300,000 Euros – 8%
- Garages up to 30,000 Euros – 7%
- Garages more than 30,000 Euros – 8%

Extremadura

- Up to 240,000 Euros – 7%
- 240,001 to 360,000 Euros – 8%
- 360,001 to 600,00 Euros – 9%
- More than 600,000 – 10%

Álava -Navarra -Vizcaya

- One tax rate only - 6%

Canarias (Canary Islands)

- One tax rate only – 6.5%

Aragón – Baleares (Balearic Islands) – Castilla y León – Castilla La Mancha – Comunidad Valenciana – Galicia – Guipúzcoa – La Rioja – Madrid – Murcia

- One tax rate only – 7%

Cataluña (Catalunya, Catalonia)

- One tax rate only – 8%

Appendix B: Spanish Lawyers in the UK

IF YOU are in the United Kingdom, you may prefer to deal with a Spanish lawyer with UK offices. One reason is that they can be useful for making a Power of Attorney should you need one unexpectedly or if it was not possible when you were in Spain itself.

Fernando Scornik Gerstein
Contact: Alberto Perez Cedillo
193-197 High Holborn
London WC1 7BD
Tel: +34 (0)207 404 8400
Fax: +34 (0)207 404 8500
Email:cedillo@:fscornik.co.uk

J Polanco Abad & Asociados
5-7 Folgate Street
London E1 6BX
Tel: +34 (0)207 377 8088
Email: demisgpol@aol.com

Chebsey & Co
51 London End
Beaconsfield
Buckinghamshire HP9 2HW
Tel: +34 (0)1494 670440
Fax: +34 (0)1494 670276
Email: pje@chebsey.com or drm@chebsey.com

Maria Dolton
El Pinar, St Raphaels
Buxted
Uxfield
East Sussex TN22 4JS
Tel/fax: +34 (0)1825 733536

Glossary of Terms

Abogados Lawyers/Solicitors.

Administrador de Finca Administrator of Land. An accountant who deals with paying taxes and keeping accounts for a *Comunidad de Propietarios,* Community of Owners. Usually known as simply 'The Administrator'.

Agente de Propiedad Inmobiliaria (API) An estate agent qualified in estate agency law and who has an official API registration number.

AGM Annual General Meeting.

Ambulatorio Cottage hospital.

Apostille An Apostille Certificate. An internationally recognised official seal legalising documents such as Power of Attorney.

Arrendamiento Lease, leaseholders, sitting tenants.

Asesor Fiscal Accountant.

Asociacion Provincial de Instaladore Association of Registered Electricians & Plumbers. Always use registered tradesmen by preference.

Ayuntamiento Town Hall, local council, local authority. There is a also a provincial authority (*Diputacion*) for the county/state, and a regional authority (*Junta*). I live in Nerja in Málaga province in Andalucía region. So my tiers of 'local' government are *Ayuntamiento de Nerja, Diputación Provincial de Málaga,* and *Junta de Andalucía.* They affect planning, building, environment, taxes, business, health services, education, culture and transport.

Boletín de Instalación A certificate issued by the electricity and water boards approving installation of electricity and water. Needed to obtain electric and water meters for new buildings.

Boletín Oficial del Estado An official state bulletin publicising legal documents

Cámara de la Propiedad Register of rented property.

Cargas Charges.

Valor Catastral Rateable value as set by the town hall.

Certificado de Fin de Obra Certificate that the architect or developer must give you on building completion to declare it at the Notary's office.

Certificado Descriptivo y Grafico Con Lindero A certificate from the *Recaudación Provincial,* provincial rates office, showing the official boundaries and registered square metres of a plot of land.

Certificado Negativo 'Negative' Certificate.

Cesion Rental contract for business premises.

CompraVenta Purchase/Sale. Basically the Contract of Sale for a property.

Comunidad de Propietarios A Community of Owners with a President, Treasurer and Secretary dealing with everyday running of the estate, complex or apartment block. You belong to it by law.

Consejería de Agricultura y Pesca Department of Agriculture & Fisheries at a Junta, the Regional Government.

IBI or Impuestos sobre Bienes Inmuebles Annual property rates paid through the local *Recaudacion Provincial* (see below).

Copia Simple A copy of the original *Escritura* title deed, but without signatures. It is sufficient to prove ownership and to arrange a bank loan.

Cortijo A farmhouse. This is the house on a *Finca.*

Cuenta Ajena Working as an employee.

Cuenta Propia o Autónomo Self employed status.

Declaración de Obra Nueva Declaring a new building. You go to the Notary's office to make an *Escritura* declaring that you have built a dwelling on land that you own. If it is a new property but already built, this declaration can be done at the same time as the *Escritura* for the land.

Delegacion de Industria Delegation of Industry, the authority which issues the certificate for the installation of the electric and water meters.

Departamento de Extranjero Foreigners' Department at the National police station where NIE numbers and residence cards are applied for.

Departamento de Urbanismo Planning Department of the Town Hall

Embargo A charge registered at the Land Registry for unpaid debts. It can be actioned by a court order to auction off property to recover debt.

Empadronamiento Electoral register.

Escritura Deeds for the property

Expediente de Dominio Document of proof of ownership, issued by the courts in the event that there is no *Escritura* for a property.

Finca A farm. Often people refer to their Finca, meaning they have a house in the country, with land

Gestoría A college registered person (GA) dealing with official paperwork, such as applications for *Residencia*, work permits, driving licences, transferring vehicle ownership, taxes etc. A person working here is a *Gestor*.

Gestoría Intermediario de Promociones y Edificaciones (GIPE) Registered Estate Agent.

Graduado Social Specialist in social security and labour laws.

Grua The tow truck that takes your car to the pound if you park wrongly, or the vehicle that rescues you when you break down on the Motorway.

Hipoteca Mortgage.

Hogar de Pensionistas Pensioners' Club or Day Centre.

Impuesto de Circulación Road Tax

Impuesto sobre Transmisiones Patrimoniales The transfer tax for transferring property to your name at the Land Registry.

INEM Unemployment and Employment Offices.

Informe Urbanistico A document from the Town Hall detailing what they will allow to be built on a given piece of land.

Inspección Técnica de Vehiculos (ITV) MOT

Impuesto sobre el Valor Añadido (IVA) Value added tax *(VAT)*

Jefatura de Costas Governmental department in charge of the coastal areas of Spain.

Junta The Regional Government. Junta de Andalucía for example.

Ley de Costa Coastal Building Laws.

Licencia de Apertura Opening Licence for a business.

Licencia de Obra A building licence which must be obtained from the Planning Department at the local Town Hall for all building work.

Licencia de Primera Ocupación Licence of First Occupation, aka the *Cédula de Habitabilidad*. Obtained from the local Town Hall which must previously have seen the *Certificado de Fin de Obra* (Building Completion Certificate). Without this licence you cannot get an electric meter.

Licencia Fiscal Fiscal Licence.

Memoria de Calidades Building specifications.

NIE (Número Identificación Extranjero) An obligatory personal and tax identification number for foreign residents in Spain.

Nota Simple A document issued by the Land Registry: a photocopy of the registration details of a property showing the present owner and if there are any mortgages or other debts on the property.

Patrimonio Wealth Tax.

Permiso de Circulación A white card authorising a vehicle to be driven on the road.

Plus Valía Local tax payable on sale of property. It is a percentage of the increase of the value of the land since it was purchased by the vendors.

Poder Power of Attorney. This will be required if you are unable to attend the Notary's Office to sign the public *Escritura* title deed.

Precio de Compra Price of Purchase.

Notario Public notary: a government appointed lawyer who legalises documents including *Escrituras* and Powers of Attorney. Highly qualified and has the same status as a judge.

Recaudación Provincial The provincial rates office which is sometimes physically located at the local Town Hall.

Rejas Iron bars on windows.

Residencia Residency. Having *Residencia* means you have a document authorising you to live in Spain permanently with the same rights and (most) responsibilities as a Spanish citizen.

Rustico/Regadio Irrigated farm land.

Secano Dry land.

Segregación Legal segregation - for example, of the plot of land that you are buying from the rest of the land on the estate.

Seguridad Social Equivalent to the UK Department of Work & Pensions.

Seguro Decenal 10 year structural insurance for a property.

Tarjeta de Inspección Técnica Equivalent to a log book for a vehicle.

Testamento Will & Testament.

Tráfico Traffic Department where driving licences etc are issued.

Traspaso/Cesión Leasehold property.

Usufructo Legal term signifying a right to use a property. For example, you may buy a property for your children but have a legal right to use it while you live.

Valor Castastral Rateable value of a property set by the Town Hall.

Lightning Source UK Ltd.
Milton Keynes UK
UKOW06f0144170715

255302UK00001B/40/P